Also by Sandra Anne Taylor

Quantum Success

Secrets of Success

Truth, Triumph, and Transformation

28 Days to a More Magnetic Life

Hay House Titles of Related Interest

BOOKS

Gratitude: A Way of Life, by Louise L. Hay and Friends

The Love Book, by John Randolph Price

A Relationship for a Lifetime: Everything You Need to Know to Create a Love That Lasts, by Kelly E. Johnson, M.D.

Relationship Problem Solver, by Kelly E. Johnson, M.D.

Rising in Love: Opening Your Heart in All Your Relationships, by Alan Cohen

CARD DECK

MarsVenus Cards, a 50-Card Deck by John Gray

All of the above are available at your local bookstore, or may be ordered by visiting:

Hay House USA: **www.hayhouse.com**®
Hay House Australia: **www.hayhouse.com.au**
Hay House UK: **www.hayhouse.co.uk**
Hay House South Africa: **www.hayhouse.co.za**
Hay House India: **www.hayhouse.co.in**

Secrets of Attraction

The Universal Laws of Love, Sex, and Romance

Sandra Anne Taylor

HAY HOUSE, INC.

Carlsbad, California • New York City
London • Sydney • Johannesburg
Vancouver • Hong Kong • New Delhi

Published and distributed in the United States by: Hay House, Inc.: www.hayhouse.com • *Published and distributed in Australia by:* Hay House Australia Pty. Ltd.: www.hayhouse.com.au • *Published and distributed in the United Kingdom by:* Hay House UK, Ltd.: www.hayhouse.co.uk • *Published and distributed in the Republic of South Africa by:* Hay House SA (Pty), Ltd.: • www.hayhouse.co.za • *Distributed in Canada by:* Raincoast: www.raincoast.com • *Published in India by:* Hay House Publishers India: www.hayhouse.co.in

Editorial supervision: Jill Kramer • *Design:* Charles McStravick

Library of Congress Cataloging-in-Publication Data

Taylor, Sandra Anne.
    Secrets of attraction : the universal laws of love, sex, and romance / Sandra Taylor
        p. cm.
    ISBN 1-56170-817-8 (tradepaper)
    1. Man-woman relationships. 2. Sexual attraction. 3. Love. 4. Self-help techniques.
    I. Title.

    HQ801 .T34 2001
    306.7—dc21

                                      2001016922

ISBN 13: 978-1-56170-817-8
ISBN 10: 1-56170-817-8

14 13 12 11   16 15 14 13
1st printing, September 2001
13th printing, January 2011

Printed in the USA

⚜ ⚜ ⚜

This book is dedicated to
my dear love, Benjamin Earl Taylor, Jr.
Also to every loving heart who seeks to share that love
with others, and every lonely heart who longs for it.

⚜ ⚜ ⚜

❧ CONTENTS ❧

❦ ACKNOWLEDGMENTS ❧

I FEEL SUCH A DEEP SENSE of appreciation to so many, but I especially want to express my gratitude to the following:

— First and foremost, to the Divine Creative Force who lives in all things and loves in all ways.

— Next, to my incredible family: Anna Salvaggio, dearest grandmother who helped with the title of this book; Sarah Marie Klingler, fun friend and generous mother; Sharon Klingler, twin heart who taught me about Spirit; Benjamin Earl Taylor, Jr., wise, funny, and very supportive husband; and the children from whom I learned about playfulness: Vica, beautiful daughter; Jenyaa, wonderful son; and Devin, dear nephew and "other son." You have all taught me so much about courage.

— To the friends of my heart, Mar Verbus, Barb Van Rensselaer, Ed Coughanor, Melissa Matousek—who gave me the book that started it all, and Julianne Stein—whose editorial advice was invaluable.

— To my colleagues Art Hardy, Michael L. Freedman, and Tom Cratsley, friends and phenomenal counselors all!

— To all of my clients—every one of whom has been a teacher—thank you.

— To Rhonda Lamvermeyer, angel-typist.

— To those who have inspired me: First, Gary Zukav, who started me on this journey with his book *The Dancing Wu Li Masters;* along with two other quantum physics writers, Michael Talbot and Nick Herbert, and to the brilliant scientists and incomprehensible minds that they wrote about, including, but not limited to: John Stewart Bell, David Bohm, Niels Bohr, Louis De Broglie, Albert Einstein, Werner Heisenberg, Max Planck, Karl Pribram, Rupert Sheldrake, and John Von Neumann. Read anything by or about these men and you will be stunned!

— And to Deepak Chopra, Wayne Dyer, Donna Eden, Louise Hay, Shad Helmstetter, Belleruth Naparstek, and Terry Cole-Whittaker. Read anything by these people and you will be inspired.

— To my support and inspiration from higher vibrations, Ronald Klingler, Rudy Staurbringer, Charles Salvaggio, Florence Bolton, dear Anthony, Raphael, Jude, and most Holy Spirit.

— Finally, to you who reads these words, I send my gratitude and love. May God bless you always.

❧ ❧ ❧

❧ Introduction ❧

THE POWER OF THE UNIVERSE is surging through you. There are actually particles within you that once took part in the formation of a star. You receive and create explosions of energy every moment of your life—this is your quantum truth. The Universe works with your own energy, and how it responds to you will depend on the precise type of energy you create. When you align yourself with the Universal energy, all of the power and wisdom of life is available to you.

The energetic action that I talk about in this book is based on some fundamental quantum principles, the most basic of which is the duality of wave and particle. When it was discovered that particles project waves of energy, and that waves of light could also be measured as particles, it rocked the world of classical physics. This book explores how this energetic phenomenon of the physical world can actually influence the way we connect on a personal level.

So much of quantum physics concerns itself with relationships: the relationship between consciousness and reality; here and there; energy and matter; wave and particle. There have been incredible discoveries concerning these relationships in the quantum world. What I've tried to do in the pages of this book is to apply those findings to the field of human experience—*human relationships.* After all, we humans are made up of the same "quantum stuff."

I was introduced to the study of quantum physics nearly 20 years ago. A friend gave me a copy of *The Dancing Wu Li*

Masters by Gary Zukav, which set me on a path that changed my life. I subsequently read every book on quantum physics that I could get my hands on. I saw that there was magic in our energetic world, and I felt that this magic could be tapped.

I've been a counselor for 22 years, and I saw that certain conclusions of quantum thought, such as "consciousness created reality," could have direct application to the psychological process. When I started to teach these principles to my clients, the results were amazing. People were able to turn their lives around more quickly because they could see the source of their problems in energetic terms. This was especially true for relationships. In fact, someone once called me an "energetic matchmaker," because the techniques I teach in my seminars and counseling sessions have brought so many people together.

But this book isn't only about success in love, it's about success in *life*. The Universal Laws discussed here apply to all levels of seeking. *All* of the experiences and situations you attract, including career and financial success, are subject to the energetic workings of the Universe. If you work with these principles and understand the kind of power they bring to your life, there's no end to the great things that you can manifest.

I myself used these concepts to connect with a fantastic and fun-loving man, who has since become my husband; I also employed these principles in adopting my two wonderful children. The power of these laws have brought me job opportunities, great friends, supportive help from the Universe, and most important, incredible peace and joy—this is my hope for you. It's my deepest desire that this book will provide insights and techniques that can help you connect with the immeasurable energetic power within and around you.

Continue to apply these principles until you see the results you're looking for. Be patient—there's a wisdom and a timing to the Universal energy. When you start to see the benefits, you'll never want to give these practices up . . . so don't! Instead, make them a way of life. They work with a strength and consistency that will change just about everything for you.

Read this book with an open heart. In many chapters, you'll find a section called "Change Your Energy Now," which is designed to give you specific ways to apply these principles. Action and affirmation will excite your energy and bring about results.

When you read this book a second time, you'll find yourself picking up on things you may not have even noticed before. In fact, every time you set a goal, let yourself review the principles once more. There's a Universe full of energy at your disposal. Make sure you stay plugged in!

There are a few technicalities that I'd like to address. The first is a grammatical one. There are countless sentences in this book that refer to "you and your partner." Since this book is written for both men and women, this created a very difficult situation with personal pronouns. (For example, the grammatically correct form of the following sentence would read: "Loving your partner means honoring him or her and balancing his or her needs with yours.") You can see how just a few paragraphs of that kind could get very tedious. Because there would be literally thousands of these cases, I opted to use the third person plural (instead of singular) to imply a generic gender. I want to clarify that the use of the plural in no way suggests multiple partners!

I also want to address the use of the words *positive* and *negative*. In scientific terms, of course, these words don't denote "good" or "bad"; they just refer to electrical charges with varying amounts of electrons. However, when I use the phrases "positive and/or negative energy," I'm referring to *your personal energy,* generally meaning beneficial or problematic energies. Since this book is also concerned with the science of energy, I felt I needed to make this distinction.

There are places where I mention specific quantum principles or theories by name without going into long, detailed scientific explanations. I do this so that anyone who's interested in investigating the technicalities further has a place to start. My main concern is with the human application of these theories, but I would encourage anyone who feels the urge to do so to study the scientific background as well.

Finally, the word *Universe* is capitalized throughout the book. I define the Universe as bigger and more creative than what is considered to be the Universe of space. I see it as the *Source* of what we call the spacial Universe, the Infinite Mind, the Creator—God.

I also believe that this Divine Consciousness is a part of everything in the cosmos, and that we're all connected, always engaging in its miraculous energy. When something happens to one, it happens to all who share its consciousness. We can't separate ourselves—either from the Universe itself or from any other thing in it.

Separation is our biggest source of suffering—from our own loving spirit, from the Divine Mind, and from each other. When we see that each of us is connected, one with everyone in the Universe, we'll finally see the end of suffering. When we choose to love, we honor our connection and excite the most dynamic energy the Universe has to offer, finally arriving at the peace we've been looking for.

It's with joy and appreciation that I offer this book to you, a loving intention to help us all move back to that peace and love—which is our Source.

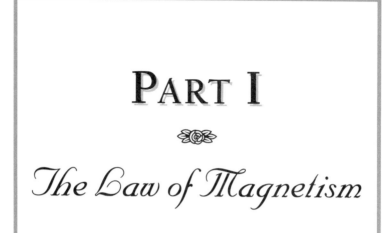

PART I

❧🌹❧

The Law of Magnetism

*"Your creative ability originates in the unseen mind.
It begins in the unseen world of waves and energy."*
— Dr. Wayne W. Dyer

All of life is an exchange of energy. Patterns of attraction *always* operate through the movement of energy. Everything that happens to us—from a passing critical remark to an exciting proposal of marriage, from a flat tire to a promotion with a huge raise—is a direct result of the energetic frequencies that we generate every day.

All of the consequences within our life are born out of the resonance of our life. Every single moment, we face an energetic option that shapes our future. When we master this principle, we can move to a new level of *consciously* creating our own destiny.

❧ CHAPTER ONE ❧

The Source of Love

"Someday, after we have mastered the winds, the
waves, the tides, and gravity, we shall harness for God
the energies of love. Then for the second time in the
history of the world, man will have discovered fire."
— Pierre Teilhard de Chardin

Are you tired of repeating the same old relationship patterns over and over again? Does it seem that no matter what you do to try to change things, the result is always the same—you're left with those familiar old feelings of loneliness, anger, hurt, and frustration? Or maybe you never seem to meet anyone at all, and if you *do*, it's pretty clear from the beginning that the affair isn't going to go anywhere. Either way, you feel you're destined to live your life in relationship limbo, always waiting and wondering why.

Well, don't give up hope. Your power to change your destiny is in your own energetic nature. No matter how long it's been since you've had a healthy relationship—even if you've *never* had one—the power, passion, and intimacy of real love are definitely available to you.

In fact, whether you realize it or not, there's a gold mine of love right in your own backyard. But in order to unearth its riches, you must first know exactly what love is, where it comes from, and how it works in the Universe. Your destiny depends on embracing the magnetic laws of attraction, for without this understanding, you'll keep mining for love in all the wrong places, always ending up with fool's gold.

Love's Form

Love's form is energy. It's one of the life-generating frequencies that move swiftly and freely through time and space. The Universe is alive with energy. Light, sound, movement—all of life takes part in an ongoing dance of energy at play. From the motion of the planets to the smallest encounters between passing strangers, everything contributes to the constant flow and exchange of personal and Universal energy.

Contrary to what most people believe, love is so much more than a feeling or a condition of a relationship. *Love is energy.* In fact, it's the greatest and most creative power in the cosmos. It may not be as immediately noticeable as the energy of sound, or as easily measurable as that of light, but love is as vital and dynamic as any energy that we're capable of experiencing.

In ancient Greek mythology, Eros, the God of Love, was originally perceived as a cosmic force—more energy than entity—whose job it was to organize and direct all of the elements of the Universe in order to create harmony out of chaos. Only later did this force become personified in the figure of the arrow-shooting angel who directed the dreams of human desire.

This organizing force is an apt representation, for it's love that's responsible for the laws that bring order to all of life. In fact, it's the energy of original love—Divine Love—that's responsible for life itself. It's the creative source of everything we see. Every person, being, or object in the Universe is an expression of the power and creativity of Divine Love.

This remarkable power is an irrepressible river of energy

that continually flows through the Universe. *You* are a part of that river. You have that Divine power radiating to and through you. It's what you do with this power that determines your destiny in relationships—and in everything else.

You can connect with this powerful river of energy through your motivation or intention. Ultimately, you must align your own intention with that of love, in order to ride that wonderful tide of amour. If you don't, you'll continue to find yourself struggling against the current.

This is what happened to Psyche, Eros's lover, when she allowed her love to turn to fear. Theirs is a classic love story, full of passion, jealousy, and suspicion; yet today, it remains an accurate representation of the patterns and the power behind the Universal Laws of love.

Eros and Psyche

Psyche was a strikingly beautiful woman, so enchanting that the people of her father's kingdom started giving her the praise they'd previously heaped on Aphrodite, the Goddess of Love. This enraged Aphrodite, so she ordered her son, Eros, to punish Psyche. Before Eros could carry out his mother's wishes, however, an oracle warned Psyche's father, telling him that the only way to appease the Love Goddess would be to abandon Psyche on top of a mountain that was inhabited by a monster.

Psyche was terrified, but she honored her father's wishes. She waited, frightened and alone, unaware that Eros was on his way to torment her. But even Eros didn't know what was to happen next. Whether due to her extraordinary beauty, or just an accidental prick of his own arrow, Eros fell madly and immediately in love with Psyche. Instead of tormenting her, he had the West Wind lift her up and carry her to his castle.

Eros placed one condition on their love. He didn't reveal

his identity to her, and he demanded that Psyche never see his face. Although this seemed to be an unusual condition, Psyche agreed, and she and Eros lived very happily together. Eros had told Psyche that if she promised never to try to cast her eyes upon him, she would be well taken care of, and her every desire would be met. Although Eros left each morning before dawn and came home only under the cover of darkness, Psyche was actually very content. She spent each evening with her tender and loving husband, and each day she lived like a princess in the castle she now called home.

In time, however, she became bored during the day. She decided to invite her sisters for a visit, partially to distract herself, and partially to show off her wealth and happiness to them. Her sisters, however, weren't impressed. Envious and resentful, they tried to find things wrong with Psyche's life. They told her that if she wasn't allowed to see her husband, it must mean that he was an ugly, hideous beast. She responded that he was far too gentle and loving to be a monster, but they continued to nag at her until Psyche herself began to lose faith.

In a moment of weakness, while Eros was sleeping, Psyche lit a lamp to check out her husband. To her delight, she saw not a monster, but the beautiful face of the God of Love. In her excitement, however, she spilled some hot oil from the lamp onto his shoulder, waking him up. Eros was appalled by this betrayal and disappeared—taking the castle and everything in it with him—leaving Psyche alone on a desolate mountain.

❧❦❧

Psyche had lost faith. She had everything she could desire, yet it wasn't enough. When she began to be motivated by doubt and fear, she lost the love that was so dear to her. This is the classic response of the laws of love. Real love *cannot* be cultivated or protected in an environment of fear. Fear suffocates the love that may be present and sabotages the pursuit of love elsewhere. If you want to create love in your life, you must look at your motivations and the feelings they create. Your intention of fear must be replaced by an intention of trust and love.

Love's Intention

Love's ultimate intention is to expand at every point of passage, and given even the smallest opportunity to do so, it will—from its origin (God) to its destination (your own heart).

> *Because your heart is its first point of passage,*
> *love's penetrating power makes one very specific demand*
> *of you—to tap into its full potential, you must begin*
> *your search for love within yourself, in your own being,*
> *in your own life. All mystical laws are founded on this*
> *basic truth:* You must begin within. *Only within*
> *yourself will you find the source of all of your intentions.*
> *And your intention is the starting point of your destiny.*

How you feel about yourself determines your intention. In fact, every emotion, word, or deed that you generate is fed by your self-perception. Without love of self, there can be no power to extend outward toward others, to kindle the flames of mutual recognition and joy. Without self-trust, you'll find yourself focusing only on what you lack, constantly living in doubt and assumed limitation. In such an environment, love's intention to expand will be always be blocked by your own perception of limitation. Your isolation is unwittingly self-inflicted, caused by your refusal to *provide for yourself the very thing you're so desperate to receive from others.*

Beliefs based in fear and self-hate dismiss the Divine, spiritual presence within you. This disconnects you from your real power, making you feel lost and alone. In such a state, you begin to desperately reach outside of yourself for another person to provide the solution. This desperation actually repels the love that you're seeking, creating within you a darkness of spirit that, like a black hole, sucks the joy out of every experience and relationship you may encounter.

As a result, anything good that's waiting to come your way is distorted, overlooked, or even driven away by your own negativity. The momentum of your life is stuck in the energetic blockage of pessimism. This heavy, stuck energy clogs the channel that connects you to love's unending sea, constricting the free-flow of real love that could be moving into your life.

But you don't have to stay stuck forever, or even for very long. By breaking down the barriers of hate in all that you experience, you'll make an energetic shift in your own momentum, which will open you up to the current of love and connect you with its energetic flow.

The fact is, the choice to hate anything—even your-self—reveals your *true* intention. The Universe is saddened by your choice, but it honors your intention and directs the river of love to flow elsewhere.

This is what happened to Psyche. She embraced fear and paid the price with the loss of her love. In time, she did get a second chance, but not before she was subjected to a number of difficult ordeals, including a horrifying descent into hell. She bore each one, though, never giving up her determination to love again. In fact, on many occasions, her determination and her renewed faith inspired Divine assistance in dealing with her difficulties.

Eventually Eros was moved by her resoluteness and love. Even Aphrodite couldn't resist the strength of her love and the purity of her newfound character. She was secured a place in heaven—where she married Eros and spent an eternity in love.

We can all have a second chance at love. But we must

first make the choice to let go of fear and learn to live with courage and self-reliance, no matter what dark times we may have to pass through. It's through this decision that we can finally enlist the powerful assistance of the spiritual laws, just as Psyche repeatedly received the help of the gods.

This decision to let go of fear is critical if you want to experience real love in your life. Your strength of character—your relationship with yourself—is the starting point of your personal and spiritual energy. All other relationships in your life mirror your attitude toward yourself. In fact, it's your relationship with yourself that determines the quality of virtually every experience that comes your way. This is true whether you're seeking romantic love, more kindness from your boss, a wider circle of friends, or even financial success.

Be clear about this: Try as you may, you won't be able to run away from this truth. There's no outside component you need to be concerned with now. *You control the light and joy that comes into your life.* Without starting at the self, the current of love will continue to flow past you, and the happiness that you seek will remain a distant dream.

The Power Source

The great, cosmic force of love is like water rushing out from a dam, generating power for miles around. Your heart is the substation for this vast power—the choice to create love within yourself releases the power, lighting up your own life and the lives of all those around you. If you refuse to cherish and honor yourself, the power of love is all dammed up within you, stagnating inside while everything around you dries up. In spite of the great accumulation of love right there at your disposal, you're unable to bring value or energy to yourself or any endeavor of your life.

The Universal Laws demand that you engage in genuine self-love, honoring who and what you are. This isn't just a vague ideal; it's based in the quantum mechanics of your own consciousness. Your *energy* determines your reality: Understanding this is the key to unleashing the powerful force of love in your life. Without it, the energy of love turns into the energy of fear and lack, contaminating you with other feelings that many confuse with love, such as neediness, desperation, control, and acquisition.

These sorts of toxic feelings and behavior patterns arise when you try to *make* love happen in your life. But, as we shall see, being needy or desperate *never* succeeds in making real love happen. Such approaches poison your energy, sabotage your efforts, and actually shut you off from the genuine experience of love.

In the following chapters, it will become very clear how your own choices have created your relationship experiences, and how you yourself have determined whether or not to allow love in. You'll see how you may have unknowingly been working against—rather than with—the laws of love, those unassailable and mystical forces that the Universe itself obeys.

These laws of love are impartial, inescapable, and absolute. Their energy moves through physical reality and manifests itself in very real ways, every day of your life. You can no more escape their impact on your personal life than you can escape the physical consequences of the law of gravity—dismissing the principles of these Universal Laws would be just as disastrous.

Of course you wouldn't ignore the law of gravity. If you walked off the second story of a building, you wouldn't be surprised to find yourself severely injured. By the same token, if you constantly ignore the Universal Laws and behave in ways that defy their demands, wondering why you keep getting hurt in love would make absolutely no sense.

When you familiarize yourself with these laws, you'll find that they empower, rather than hurt, you. Like your understanding of gravity, if you're willing to embrace the laws of love, you can finally stop your relationships from crashing to the ground.

❧ CHAPTER TWO ❧

Quantum Attraction

*"From every human being there rises a light that
reaches straight to heaven, and when two souls that
are destined to be together find each other, the streams
of light flow together and a single brighter light goes
forth from that united being."*
— Ba'al Shem Tov

The first Universal Law that directly impacts your experience of romantic love is the **Law of Magnetism,** which reveals the patterns of energies moving and relating to each other in the Universe. In fact, this is the primary source of *all* that you experience. *It's an energetic, not romantic, phenomenon,* a very real force of nature that influences your life on a daily basis. Every single part of your destiny, relationship or otherwise, is determined by the action of this law in your life.

Your Magnetic Vibration

At one time, it was believed that matter and energy manifested separately, completely unrelated to each other. Quantum physics has revealed, however, that *everything*—all of life, from the solid mass of the earth to every object and being on it—pulses with energetic frequencies. *You,* the people and places around you, even this book—all resonate with energy. And that energy moves outward from you, in space and time, attracting and responding to the other energy in the cosmos.

When objects vibrating at similar frequencies come together, their frequencies actually begin to match. This is true for you and your environment, too—sometimes your frequency harmonizes with the slow, methodical "heartbeat" of the earth's energy; sometimes it aligns with the rapid, pounding frequency of a song on the radio. There are even times when your frequency resonates with the agitated, fearful, or depressed energy that someone around you may be projecting. This phenomenon is called *entrainment,* and it's one of the quantum physical truths that stimulate the Law of Magnetism.

> *The Law of Magnetism states that each of us creates and projects a certain kind of energy—an actual frequency. And we attract and resonate to the exact same kind of energy that we send out. In short, the Law of Magnetism is the ongoing process of transmitting and receiving energy, an energy that's generated by and about ourselves.*

We're engaged in this process of transmitting and receiving every moment of our lives. Based on our attitudes, perceptions, actions, and beliefs, we constantly project a tangible, even palpable energy. That energy resonates at very specific frequencies, moving outward from us, usually without any awareness on our part. Eventually, the vibrations that we send out return to us in the form of the people we meet and the situations we attract.

In fact, if we pay close attention to the patterns of our lives, we'll find that it's unerringly and persistently true that *the energy we keep magnetizing from the world is exactly the same energy that we've generated from within.* Whatever we

believe or feel about ourselves—or however we energetically express ourselves—we will inevitably attract the same
in return.

Whether we're aware of it or not, this truth applies to
everything that we draw into our lives, including jobs, money,
and the quality of all of our relationships. It's in our romantic relationships, however, where the Law of Magnetism is
most keenly felt and most readily apparent. If we want to
increase the amount of love in our lives, therefore, it will be
necessary to investigate what kind of loving (or unloving)
energy we're unconsciously creating, and how the Law of
Magnetism is responding to it.

The Focus of Love

There are two important components of the Law of
Magnetism. The first is this: **Our magnetic attraction is
based largely upon how we value and treat *ourselves*,
not just on how we value or treat others.** The fact is,
without a genuine valuing of self, it's virtually impossible to
value others or be valued by them.

Many people are under the misconception that if they
just treat others well enough, they'll be treated well in
return. Yet there are countless stories of people who have
been excessively kind to others and have still been treated
badly. In fact, it's a common paradox that the more desperate
some people are to please others, the worse they themselves
get treated—even to the point of abuse.

This isn't, of course, an encouragement to be unkind to
others. But if we don't base our kind treatment of others
upon a healthy reverence for ourselves, then that care, as loving as it may *seem*, doesn't resonate with love at all.

Without self-love at its source, our charity toward others is really a manipulation, based in fear, guilt, or the need
to be accepted. In accordance with the law, this energy

inevitably magnetizes unhappiness and unloving responses, because it's based in unhappiness at its source. So, no matter how kind or loving the act may appear, if the motivating source is negative, then the consequence will be likewise.

The motivating source of your energy is your underlying intention. It's the motivation behind your choices, not the choices themselves, that create the resonant frequencies you project. No matter what the nature of the decision is, it's actually the intention behind it that permeates your energetic field.

When you're being kindhearted, purely out of the intention to be loving and supportive, then your kindness will truly resonate with love, and you'll be treated lovingly in return. If you find yourself consistently being treated badly in spite of your altruism, however, you'd better *honestly* investigate your own intention again—you could have a more subtle, but still manipulative, motivation that you may not be aware of.

For example, a client of mine named Shirley was one of the most generous, sensitive, and giving people that I'd ever known. Although she often found herself resenting it, she did anything and everything that anyone asked of her. Yet she could never understand why her efforts were never really appreciated. In fact, the more she did for others, the more they took advantage of her. People were using her, and many even treated her cruelly.

Shirley assumed that she was doing nice things for people out of a genuine desire to help, and I'm sure that this was part of her motivation. But upon further investigation, she realized that her parents had had very high expectations of her along this line, and they always gave their approval accordingly. As a result, Shirley had been compelled to please people out of a desire to gain their acceptance, and to subsequently feel better about herself.

She projected her parents' expectations onto the rest of the world, believing that this was the only way she could validate herself and raise her self-esteem. She'd felt that her intention was sincere, but it was really full of obligation, fear of rejection, and the need to be loved. Although her behavior was kind, *her energy and her motivation* was unloving toward herself, and actually manipulative to others. As a result, it was absolutely unavoidable that she'd receive unloving treatment in return.

This law demands that all of our actions be based in a genuine self-valuing—a reverence for ourselves and our lives. Then our love and kindness toward others will resonate with authenticity, tenderness, and compassion. The Universe longs to return our own love and compassion to us, but only when it stems from a genuinely loving heart is it abundantly free to do so.

The Frequencies of Love

The second and most important component of the Law of Magnetism is this: **Patterns of attraction *always* operate through the *movement of energy.*** We project energy; we attract energy—this is our physical reality. And the quality of the energy we attract will always be based on the quality of the energy we put out.

Radio and TV stations broadcast their signals at certain frequencies. When we tune our sets into the same frequency, we can pick up their signals. The closer we get to their exact frequency, the clearer the signal becomes. In a different but equally energetic way, *we* also broadcast signals about ourselves. *These are actual, energetic messages about our true nature, our deepest held beliefs, and even our unspoken attitudes.* And they'll be picked up and felt by everyone around us.

We all know people who are stimulating, fun, easygoing, and enjoyable to be with. When we're with them, we feel better about ourselves, and when we leave them, we feel satisfied, as if we've been given something to take with us. These are the energy boosters of the world—they send out "happy signals" because they're happy with themselves.

We also know people who are definitely *not* fun to be around. There's a heaviness to their presence, an agitation to their energy. And they often leave us feeling dissatisfied and drained, as if something has been taken away, instead of given to us. These are the energy vampires. They send out hateful signals because, no matter how they may behave, they're inwardly hateful to themselves.

Surprisingly, the reactions we have to them aren't just vague feelings, they're real energetic responses. We have these reactions to people because we come in contact with their **personal energy field.** They may not need to say or do anything obvious to warrant such a response, but their energy is unmistakable. Based upon the frequency of the love in their own hearts, and on the predominant force of their own beliefs, they have the power to give us energy or to take it away, to attract us or repel us. It's an *energetic* connection.

You, too, have your own personal energy field that you broadcast yourself. It constantly emanates outward from you, created by the mental, physical, and emotional energy of your life. It's this personal energy field that determines *everything* you attract. Like the reception of radio signals, the kind of people who tune into and respond to you most strongly will be those that resonate most clearly with your own frequencies.

People with similar feelings, needs, and beliefs are the ones that are attracted to your signals, the ones you'll magnetize and draw closer to you. These people resonate to your own particular frequency because, although they may express them very differently, they have the same negative or positive energies within their own hearts. This is why it's so important to understand exactly what kind of energy you're broadcasting in and about your life.

If worry or fear is the basic energy that moves outward from you, you'll undoubtedly attract equally worried or frightened people to you—some may be passive and timid, yet others may actually be abrasive and hostile. It may not seem so, but these hostile people are just as afraid as the meek ones. Their fear is about a lack of power, so they compensate for it with their bullying and arrogance.

If depression, doubt, or desperation are the significant energies you generate, even as an unspoken undercurrent to your life, then you'll magnetize depressed or depressing people, and the situations you find yourself in will cause you to become even more despondent and uncertain.

If you tend to be self-critical, it will be very easy to magnetize others who are more than willing to be critical of you, too. And if you often find yourself being criticized by others, this indicates that on some level you don't accept yourself as you are, and that you're indeed judging yourself in some way.

> *The world is a switching station that always sends your own energy back to you—this is the inescapable reality of the Law of Magnetism. In your career, financial status, home, and relationships, what you find yourself experiencing will always be an outward picture of the energy that you yourself are creating on a daily basis.*

If your partner is unavailable, either emotionally or in other ways, then you're actually living a lifestyle where *you* aren't available to yourself. How can a person not be available to oneself? It's simple. If you never encourage yourself, if you never give yourself the time to take care of your own priorities, to support yourself, or to solve your own problems, then you're actually not available to yourself. If you don't take responsibility for your life, or take action on your own behalf, then you're not available to yourself, and you'll never attract a willingness from others to do likewise.

You must ask yourself, "Do I give *myself* the time, support, and encouragement that I would expect from my partner, family, or friends? Do I talk to *myself* in ways I would like to be talked to by others? Do *I* forgive myself for my own mistakes? Do I acknowledge and appreciate *myself* the way I would hope to be appreciated and acknowledged by my friends and loved ones?"

If the answer is no, *don't expect to be treated well by the outside world.* The Law of Magnetism is always quite literal in its response to your energy.

It becomes painfully obvious then, that if you want to understand why your life and relationships are the way they are, you must first investigate the energy you're creating in and about yourself. This is an absolutely essential process.

If you want to magnetize riches, you *must* perceive the richness within yourself. If you want to magnetize the sensitivity, respect, and availability that you desire, *you* must be sensitive, respectful, and available to yourself.

If you want to magnetize the honoring and love that you deserve, you must first be willing to make choices that are honoring and loving to yourself. Until you do, you'll be destined to repeat the same old patterns, relationship after relationship—or continue to receive the same treatment in the relationship you're in now.

There's just no getting around it: Your treatment of yourself, your mental patterns, your dominant beliefs, and your emotional nature all determine your personal energy field. Everything that you do, think, and say—even the way you move and speak—projects who you are into the energetic world. That projection moves outward in waves around you, vibrating even to the remote regions of Universal space and time. Eventually your resonance comes back to you, bringing with it those situations and people that return your own emotional energy—whether you're pleased with those results or not. This is the magnetic force behind your love—and life—experience. It's the reality that only *you* generate.

Your Personal Energy Field

What's *your* personal energy like? The following quiz is designed to give you an idea of your energetic leanings. Based on your tendencies, place the appropriate numerical value next to each statement, then add up the total. Be honest!

❧

Personal Energy Quiz

Never (0)	**Half the Time (2)**	**Always (4)**
Sometimes (1)	**Most of the Time (3)**	

___1. I wake up feeling relaxed and peaceful.

___2. I look forward to the day with enthusiasm and expectation.

___3. I generally have confidence in what I do.

___4. I'm willing to take risks and try new and different things.

___5. I'm a tolerant person who rarely finds fault with others or blames them for my problems.

___6. I'm generally comfortable with my appearance.

___7. I see myself as equal to others. I deserve to be respected.

___8. I set reasonable boundaries and make reasonable requests.

___9. I tend to smile a lot. I have a playful attitude about the things I have to do.

___10. I feel comfortable expressing my feelings to most people.

___11. I enjoy being spontaneous. I see my life as an adventure.

___12. I have many different outlets for my interests and creativity.

___13. I schedule my time so that I don't have to hurry to or through things.

___14. I schedule time to spend on myself and my own goals, including quiet time.

___15. I feel a sense of purpose and direction.

___16. I appreciate the good things I have in my life, and I spend time acknowledging and enjoying them each day.

___17. My eating habits are generally healthy.

___18. I exercise regularly.

___19. I focus on what's going on now. Whatever the task, I try to enjoy what I'm doing in the present.

___20. I'm flexible with change and comfortable with the unexpected.

___21. I trust my intuition and generally let it be my guide.

___22. My words and thoughts tend to be optimistic, positive, and encouraging. I affirm and value myself in conscious ways.

___23. When something goes wrong, I face it openly. I try to see the opportunity in every situation.

___24. I let the little things take care of themselves, and trust that things will turn out okay without my needing to control or worry about everything.

___25. I interact easily with others without judging them, and without concern that they will judge me.

_____ **TOTAL** (See information below on how to score this quiz.)

Your total is your Personal Energy Quotient (PEQ), and it indicates a number of things about you: (1) It's the percentage of optimistic and peaceful energy that you tend to project in the world; (2) it represents your potential for attracting successful experiences back into your life, including healthy relationships; and (3) at its most basic level, this number represents how happy you are—the percentage of time and energy that you actually spend experiencing life in an enjoyable, fulfilling, and self-actualized way.

Your answers to this quiz will be different depending on the day and your mood, so try to take the test a few times and then average the scores. Also repeat the test in six months and again in a year to see how effectively you're integrating the changes you want to make. It's very encouraging to see how your personal energy changes according to the positive mental and emotional action you take on your own behalf.

❧

This is how the scoring works:

If your PEQ is 80 to 100 percent, you're pretty happy, and your personal energy will reflect that. You're relatively comfortable with yourself, and others are comfortable with you, too. If you fall into this category and aren't in a relationship but still desire one—or perhaps aren't getting the fulfillment out of the one you have—pay close attention to the specific items on the quiz that may be a problem. There may be only one or two issues that you need to work on—make these a priority. Even a little change in your habits can make a very big difference in your personal energy field.

If your score is 60 to 80 percent, you aren't alone. The highest amount of people polled fit into the 60 to 70 percent range of this category. You're doing okay, but if you're under 75 percent, there's definitely room for improvement. You need to work on being more spontaneous and self-honoring. You may find that you often put yourself second, so investigate your patterns thoroughly. Bring a positive attitude to your self-talk, and use the energy-changing techniques to create the peaceful resonance that attracts real love and happy outcomes.

If your score is 40 to 60 percent, you may often feel like you're just getting by. You can increase your happiness by striving less and being more flexible and forgiving of yourself. You must also establish a greater balance in your life. It will be *very* important to use the suggested tools in this book to release judgment and create a stronger, more magnetic and self-directed personal energy. Don't blow it off— *do it!* All of your efforts in this direction will increase your energy of attraction, and you'll be surprised by how the patterns of your relationships change when you're willing to work on yourself first.

If your PEQ is 20 to 40 percent, you may have been feeling greatly discouraged lately. You have feelings of self-doubt, uncertainty, and fear, and your energy shows it. Your efforts toward building a positive personal energy field through healthy self-love need to be a *top priority* to you. Keep at it. Structure *all* of these techniques into your daily routine. Don't miss a day, and it *will* pay off. Your internal changes need to be your biggest goal. Success in love and in any other external aim will follow suit.

If your score is under 20 percent, you're probably very unhappy, feeling like you're fighting your way through life. This is due to a profound insecurity that may have been part of your history—but does *not* have to remain your reality. You definitely need to let go of your fears and accept yourself in an entirely new way. Yes, it *can* be done. Set aside time each day to work on these issues. By consistently making changes in your thinking, you *will* change your energy *and* your reality. You may need to see a cognitive therapist, someone who can help you to create healthier thought patterns, but it will be well worth the effort.

Change Your Energy Now

In order to change your personal energy, all of the above statements to which you assigned a zero, one, or two value have to become *very real goals* in your life. These are the lifestyle changes that will change your energy. Engaging in these choices will make you a much happier, much more authentically empowered person.

It's true, of course, that you do not have to be happy just to attract someone. You will still be able to magnetize someone who's also unhappy and willing to share their misery with you in all sorts of interesting and unpleasant ways. But the Law of Magnetism shows that like attracts like, and if you want to attract someone who *is* happy and capable of sharing that happiness with you, you must first cultivate the ability to be happy within yourself.

So whatever your score may be, here's your first assignment: Check off *all* of the statements to which you've assigned either a zero, one, or two value. Write them down on index cards or on a separate piece of paper. Keep this list with you and *read it often*. These are the attitudes and behavioral patterns you must learn to develop if you want to create the kind of energy that will magnetize healthy and happy relationships. *Each day, use one of these statements as a personal goal for that day.* Take a card with you and practice making new choices in your daily life that will help make that statement more true for you.

For example, if you assigned a value of one (sometimes) to statement number 14 (scheduling time for your own goals), you need to look at your lifestyle to see how you could make these changes. You should actually schedule the time for your own goals on your calendar. Make a date *with* yourself *about* yourself, and soon you'll attract others who will do the same.

If your issue is taking risks (number 4) or being spontaneous (number 11), start to look for every opportunity possible to do something different, try something new, act on an intuition, or take even a little risk in your life.

These new activities may seem awkward at first, but change always feels that way. It's worth the risk, however, for the only alternative to making a change is choosing to remain the same—which, of course, creates the same energy and attracts the same results.

You can speed up this process by using each statement that you valued zero, one, or two as an **affirmation.** Repeat it many times a day. This will reinforce your new intention and continue to point you in your new direction.

For example, if you assigned a value of one to statement 3, you should tell yourself every day, *"I'm learning to have more and more confidence in the things I do."* If you assigned a value of two to *either* statement 1 or 2, go to bed each night affirming, *"I wake up every morning feeling relaxed and peaceful, looking forward to the day."* Also say it in the morning and repeat it throughout the day.

Intention supported by repetition eventually creates your truth. So use this affirmation process with every one of your zero, one, and two valued statements—and don't stop until they become a reality.

The more you change your intentions in this way, the

more you'll see the circumstances around you alter, too. Your destiny is directly linked to your energy, and your energy is largely determined by the resonance of your attitude. And—*no matter what may have been true about your past*—your present attitude is always of your own choosing.

You Are the Bottom Line

The key to your personal energy field is found in your ability to be comfortable and peaceful with who you are. Your happiness depends on this, as well as the quality of the relationships and treatment you attract—even your financial success stems from this truth. Ultimately, to achieve what you desire, you must learn to like, as well as love, yourself.

As a counselor, I've been teaching people how to like themselves for years. At first, there's always a hesitation: "Do I *really* need to do this? *Can* it really be done? How much effort will it take?" Disbelief and unwillingness to change are the most common reactions.

But when people find out that *their self-love is actually the energetic source of their destiny, and the only way to get what they truly want out of life,* they realize that it's finally time to take themselves seriously.

When was the last time *you* considered whether or not you liked yourself? It's extremely important to be on top of the potential changes in your attitude about yourself, and to find the many subtle and sometimes insidious ways your thoughts, behaviors, and self-talk may be sabotaging your inner sense of well-being—and your energy.

The extent to which you like yourself can often be a variable, subject to change, depending on such things as what you're doing, the people you're with, or even what you look like on any given day. Yet in reality, *your inherent value is never a variable*. It's a part of your identity, a constant no matter what's going on around you.

This is the crucial dynamic of the Law of Magnetism: The constancy of peaceful and healthy self-valuing is the foundation upon which your ability to value and appreciate everything else is based. If you can't appreciate yourself, it will be impossible to appreciate the trappings of your life. Even if you acquire all of the riches and relationships you desire, your lack of *self*-appreciation renders them empty and meaningless, leaving you with a lingering sense that something's missing.

But when you acknowledge and appreciate your inherent and eternal worth, you'll experience a fullness in your life, which brings about a profound appreciation for everything. This energy of profound gratitude will eventually attract even more to your life that you can appreciate.

All of your happiness will be filtered through your genuine regard for yourself, so it's imperative that you begin now to arrive at a peaceful, respectful acceptance of your own being. Even if you've never really experienced this peaceful self-acceptance, you *can* and *must* create it for yourself!

If there's something you want to change in your life, then there's something you must change in your*self*. It may not be a big thing, but there is something. You *are* the energy you "broadcast," and the people and experiences who have "tuned into" you to this point have done so for a reason. It's time to find out why.

✇ CHAPTER THREE ✇

The Resonance of Your Life

*"If thou wish to reach the perfection of love,
it befits thee to set thy life in order."*
— Catherine of Siena

The Law of Magnetism is clear. It responds directly—and in kind—to your personal energy field. As a result, you must begin by being fully aware of, *and responsible for,* everything that creates that energy. There's just no other way to change your destiny.

What exactly goes into making the energy you send out? Much more than you might realize. Energy resonates in three major ways in the physical world, and it's important to understand how you participate in every one of them.

1. The Resonance of Motion

The first type of resonance is *mechanical,* or the energy of movement. It's well known how the movement of water and wind can produce electricity—your own movement creates and projects energy, too. How much you move, as well as the way you move, plays a big part in the energy you send out.

Very few people give much thought to the way they position and move their bodies. Our daily motions have become so automatic and instinctual that most of us are hardly even aware of them. Nor do we realize the impact our movements may be having on our lives.

But if you want to change some of your old, stuck emotional patterns, you might want to consider changing your patterns of physical motion first. The fact is, *motion* and *emotion* are significantly connected, and the first is extremely important in helping to clear out the second.

The more you move, the more energy you'll have and—depending on your other resonant factors—the more pure the energy you will project. If you don't get enough movement, your beliefs and past experiences are more likely to stay stuck in both your body and personal energy field. This causes you to continue to believe and behave in the same old ways and resonate with the same old frequency. If you want to attract someone who isn't equally as stuck, then getting some major muscle movement, exercise, deep breathing, and stretching on a regular basis would be a necessary start.

The *way* you move is also an important factor in what you project. Do you walk with dignity or disinterest? Do you hold yourself with confidence or concern? Are your movements fluid and peaceful, or urgent and fragmented? If your movement is slow and dragging, you may find that things are often slow in coming to you. If your movement is too rushed and agitated, you can find yourself feeling nervous and urgent, and you'll quickly attract irritating people and experiences to you.

Spend a few days investigating your physical activity. If you spend most of your time sitting, your vital energy starts to pool around you, becoming heavy and dense. This can keep your frequency lethargic and unenthused. Keep in mind that this slow, sluggish resonance is what you'll be broadcasting, and you'll attract equally unenthusiastic responses.

*Your physical action increases your attraction.
Exercise, stretch, move, and let go. Every time you
move your body with the intention to move out your
old, unhealthy feelings and thoughts, you make a
dynamic shift in your frequencies.*

Be aware of the way you carry yourself. If you stand erect, with your head and shoulders up, you not only project an energy of confidence, but you also open up your heart center. This makes it easier to send out your own loving energy, while at the same time allowing you to be more receptive to attracting love in return.

If you slouch while you walk, always looking down and dropping your shoulders, it not only appears uninviting, but more important, it closes off your heart center. This prevents you from making the heart-to-heart connection that's so necessary in the process of loving communication. It also reduces your potential to receive the heartfelt interest that others are willing to extend to you.

Remember to move the muscles of your face. Smile as often as possible, certainly more often than you frown. Relax your forehead and eyebrow muscles; in fact, relax your entire body. Practices like yoga and tai chi are great forms of movement.

Another very important factor in your mechanical resonance is your pattern of breathing. So many people live their lives as shallow breathers, never really taking a cleansing breath at all. This actually promotes sensations of fear, anxiety, and even depression, which are three very powerful energy breakers!

Deep breathing is the movement of the internal self. Regular deep breathing calms the mind, while stimulating the circulation. This helps move old energy out on a cellular level, which is a very important process in creating a clear and attractive personal energy field. It also creates a more relaxed and inviting presence. As you exhale, affirm that you're letting go of unwanted, unhealthy energy. This engages the next two types of resonance as well.

2. The Resonance of Sound

The second type of resonance is *acoustic*, or the energy of sound. Whether you're aware of it or not, your personal energy field is affected by both the sounds that you make as well as the sounds that you surround yourself with.

What are the words you use? Are they filled with anger and hostility, or are they pleasant, peaceful, and loving? How do you use your voice? What's the melody behind your words? Is your tone sarcastic and aggressive; faltering and unsure; or confident, strong, and clear? Start to become aware of the tone and timbre of your voice. Does it change in different situations? You may even want to tape yourself to find out.

To acoustically enhance your personal energy field, speak clearly with a strong voice, one that reverberates with ease and self-confidence. Whining, talking too slowly, or slurring your speech muddies up your energy, attracting confused or depressing people and circumstances to you. Hurried and agitated speech fragments your energy and projects an abrasive frequency, attracting agitating situations and harsh people.

Your acoustic resonance amplifies your other energetic frequencies. If you verbalize your negative thoughts out loud, you're actually doubling the power of their energy. Practice saying optimistic and nurturing expressions with clear and confident tones. Use your voice to amplify your affirmative energy, and you'll broadcast a beautiful frequency.

In addition to the sounds you make, start to develop an awareness of those that you regularly expose yourself to.

Listening to soothing, inspiring, or exciting music can do wonders for your personal energy. Cut down on your TV time, especially unsettling broadcasts full of loud or violent noises. Noise is a part of our world, and some of it can't be avoided, but we need to be much more discriminating about the sounds that we *can* control.

The external acoustics in your life mingle with and influence your own energetic frequencies. If you're constantly being overstimulated by toxic sounds, it can scatter your energy and create vibrational unrest.

As a result, silence is an absolutely necessary part of your acoustic energy. It's very important to spend at least some part of your day being quiet, allowing your own energies to calm down and arrive at a quiet state of restful self-awareness. Tune out the outside world and learn how to relax with the sensations of being alone—with no noise or distractions of any kind.

This may feel uncomfortable at first because we're so used to the "white noise" going on around us. Some people are actually addicted to acoustic stimulation and need to have a radio or television on most of the time. This helps to numb their feelings, distract their thoughts, and cover up sensations such as pain and loneliness, which the silence may reveal.

If silence unnerves you, start with just a few minutes a day. Relax with it, breathe into it, and get comfortable with your own company. Since it's such an important part of your energy resonance, increase your daily quiet time as you become more comfortable with it.

Spending time in silence helps you get in touch with your true spiritual self. It creates clarity and a greater capacity to focus. This sends out waves of peaceful energy that are very calming and attractive to most people in this chaotic world.

Silence, movement, and sound are undeniable factors in determining your destiny. You must, therefore, find out how you express your energy in these ways. Then your investigation must continue on to the third type of resonance that influences your magnetic attraction.

3. The Resonance of Light

By far the greatest part of your personal energy field is *electromagnetic* in nature. This is the energy of your *light*—the light and love of your heart and mind, the life force of your eternal soul. This energy is very real, however subtle, and expresses itself in a myriad of ways, particularly in your beliefs and emotions.

> *Every thought, feeling, choice, and conclusion projects your inner light. This is the energetic essence of who you are and the resonance of your most dominant self. As a result, the source of your electromagnetic power is found in your strongest emotions, habitual behaviors, and most deeply held beliefs.*

The single most significant influence on the light (or darkness) you carry with you is your perception of yourself. In order to project the healthiest *light* energy, you must finally make the choice to love and value yourself completely. It's not arrogance you're seeking, but authentic joy and belief in your own being. Without this as your central focus, the signals you broadcast will be striving and needy. You'll constantly be looking outside of yourself for meaning and value, and this desperate energy will be a turnoff to anyone who isn't equally despairing.

People don't only respond to your overt energy, such as your words and behaviors; they react to your subtle light energy, too. No matter how hard you may try to hide it, the energy of your true feelings about your life and yourself moves outward from you. This is why your emotions play such a very big part in your electromagnetic resonance—if a thought, situation, or experience is emotionally charged, it increases the intensity of that particular vibration. Anger, rage, fear, and depression project very different frequencies than joy, love, peace, and appreciation, and they magnetize very different results. It will be incredibly important, therefore, to become aware of your most powerful and frequently experienced feelings.

It is necessary to express your feelings in order to honor and acknowledge the emotional context of your life. *You must move through your feelings so you can move them out of your frequency.* To do that, however, you first have to identify and let yourself experience them.

We often cover up our most painful feelings in order to protect ourselves from old hurts. You need to uncover and express these feelings so you no longer have to carry their energy with you. Write about them; talk them out. Let yourself feel so you can let it all go. But be careful not to wallow in negative feelings that have simply become habits. Emotions—whether good or bad—are a powerful resonance—change those feelings by changing your thinking.

Self-treatment is another important factor in your electromagnetic resonance. Since the Law of Magnetism is so exact, you must be *very precise* in your treatment of yourself. If you want to be valued by someone else, you *must* see yourself as valuable. If you want to be loved, you *must* be loving to yourself and see yourself as being *worthy* of love. If this isn't your genuine perception, then your first priority must be to *change these conclusions at all costs.*

When people ask themselves why they're not getting the relationships that they want, their assumptions are generally the same: They think it's their looks, income, or position in life. They think that they're not going to the right places in order to meet the right people. Worst of all, they think that there must be something wrong with them, some inherent defect that causes them to keep experiencing the lovelessness and loneliness that fills their lives.

None of these things is true, and it's very important not to fall into these mental traps—thinking this way will only further sabotage your efforts at love. There's only one thing missing, and it isn't your looks, money, prestige, or character. It's your *genuine understanding* of the full and real value that already exists within your true self. Rest assured that it's not your value that's missing, but your *understanding* of your value. It's not your worthiness of love that's lacking, but your *belief* in your worthiness.

Once you make this shift in your thinking, you'll be able to make the transition in your energy that will change your very destiny. The Law of Magnetism demands it; your happiness in love requires it.

Susan's Energy Shift

I once had a 32-year-old client named Susan who was very confused about why she never seemed to attract the right guys. Her experience with relationships always turned out to have the same problems: They would start out fine, but eventually the men would reveal themselves to be selfish, superficial, and often very judgmental. Susan just couldn't understand why she seemed to keep meeting the "same guy" over and over again. With each new relationship, she hoped that things would be different, yet each turned out the same way—the only change was in her varying degrees of disappointment.

She eventually came in for therapy, believing that there must be something wrong with her that caused her to keep falling into these same relationship patterns. She called herself a "jerk magnet," and was beginning to feel hopeless about ever meeting "Mr. Right."

Except for this particular problem, everything else in her life seemed to be working well. On the surface, she seemed to be very confident. She worked out and was in great shape. She had an excellent job at a large brokerage firm and got along well with most of the people at work. Yet Susan consistently felt an undercurrent of dissatisfaction, which she attributed to her romantic disappointments. But it turned out to be much more profound than that.

Upon deeper investigation, we found that the primary source of Susan's dissatisfaction was Susan herself. Without ever being aware of it, she had very subtly, yet chronically, scrutinized herself for faults and mistakes. Susan had an undercurrent of self-doubt and feelings of inadequacy that she wasn't even aware of. For instance, she'd look in the mirror and casually think things such as, "I really ought to get a nose job" or "I've got to lose some weight."

To everyone else who knew her, however, neither of these things was necessary. She would leave a social situation and think, "Why did I say that? I should have reacted differently." And if someone complimented her, instead of saying thank you and knowing she deserved it, she would always laugh it off, dismissing both the compliment and herself.

At first she was very surprised by the many subtle ways she was devaluing herself. She'd never been overtly self-deprecating, yet such reactions created a persistent tug at her self-esteem. This created a very low-level, yet chronic, depression. Although she had no conscious awareness of it, this melancholy was enough to have a significant impact on her internal light resonance.

When I explained the Law of Magnetism to Susan, she could see that her own negative energies were sabotaging her desires and attracting judgmental men. There was a darkness to her energy—but she was determined to change things.

We started cleaning up her personal energy by first cleaning up *all* of her thoughts. She spent a few weeks making a list of all of the negative things she thought about herself and her circumstances. We then replaced those negative statements with positive, healthy, self-nurturing ones, which she exposed herself to on a daily basis.

It took a while for her to get comfortable with this, but in time, Susan became a master at affirmative self-talk. She saw it as a project, much like her daily physical workout, one that she could focus on in a structured way to get the results she wanted. In time, she began to feel better about herself, and even her family and friends noticed that she seemed to be happier and more relaxed.

Susan took *full responsibility* for the creation of healthy, self-loving heart energy. She was amazed, and even somewhat amused, by how prevalent her negative thinking had been. She now prided herself on being more optimistic. Susan was able to lift her depression by changing her thoughts of dissatisfaction. No matter what happened in her life, she refused to give up. Despite two more brief repetitions of the same types of relationships that she'd been through before, she kept moving forward.

Susan was vigilant about not doubting or criticizing herself in even the smallest of ways. She also felt free to refuse to let others criticize her. Although this was very difficult at first, she soon realized that she felt much better for insisting upon it. She handled her new relationships differently, ending them early on if she didn't feel she was getting the respect that she now knew she deserved.

Her new approach paid off. About 18 months after starting to make these changes, she began a new relationship with someone at work. Although they had previously worked on several projects together, he had never asked her out before—this time he did.

Doug turned out to be just what Susan was looking for. He was strong yet supportive, fun-loving, and not at all uptight or judgmental. They dated for a year, and when they got engaged, Susan finally asked Doug why he'd waited so long to ask her out.

His response was, "There was just something different

about you before. I guess I might have been interested, but I never got around to it. Then last year, I just couldn't resist. I kept looking at you from across the room thinking, *I've got to get to know her."*

Susan's physical appearance hadn't changed—she neither got a nose job nor lost any weight—there was nothing externally different about her. The only thing that had changed was Susan's own treatment of herself. What had changed was the resonance of her internal light. She cleaned up the energy of her own heart, allowing the purity of her love—for herself and her life—to break free. She began radiating an entirely new energy. Free from judgment, and full of optimism, she was finally able to magnetize someone who could return her high spirits and pure love.

Change Your Energy Now

If you're willing to take complete responsibility for the resonance that you create, you can achieve the same results as Susan. First, you need to become *fully conscious* of the energy choices you're making now. Then you need to be *unceasingly persistent in creating only the kind of energy that you want to attract.* If that which you focus on expands, you really need to *know* what your focus is.

Keep a small notebook with you throughout the day. Divide the paper into two columns, heading them as *Positive* and *Negative*. Under each column, simply put a mark indicating every time you notice yourself engaging in each kind of thought or feeling, and at the end of each day, total the marks up.

This is just a counting exercise, designed to give you an idea of how much negative or positive energy you're creating. Don't be surprised if you find yourself having dozens, even hundreds, of negative thoughts in one day! I've had many clients express utter amazement at the amount of negative thinking they were doing before they developed an awareness of it.

Your personal energy field is like a bank account. Every moment of your waking life, you are making some kind of deposit—whether it be negative or positive, hopeless or hopeful, fearful or trusting. The kind of energy that accrues in your account depends on the energy that you yourself deposit on a moment-to-moment basis.

Don't deceive yourself about this. It all—every bit of it—adds up and makes a difference. *When it comes time to withdraw on your destiny, you will only be able to take out the same kind of energy that you've put in.* This is your magnetic truth. You can't get a positive return on a negative investment; nor can you linger in pessimism, fear, and self-criticism and then wonder why your life never gets any better. You simply cannot refuse to take any action and then complain about being stuck.

Instead, you must persistently ask yourself, "What kind of energy am I banking now? What kind of investment in my future is this thought, decision, or action creating? Is this really the energy that I want to withdraw later?"

Decide now to make only loving, joyful, and optimistic deposits. Clean up the energy that's already there, and create new and healthy energetic patterns. Do this with intention, conviction, and repetition, and you'll move toward the future amassing a fortune in many joyous and happy returns.

❧ ❧ ❧

❧ CHAPTER FOUR ❧

The Energy of Your Mind

"Man is made by his beliefs. As he believes, so he is."
— The Bhagavad Gita

Your mind is like a constantly whirring generator, per-
petually spinning out your life force in clouds of palpable energy around you. In order to change your *life,*
you must change your *life force.* And in order to change
your life force, you must change your mind.

Changing your thinking is one of the most crucial parts
of changing your personal energy. It can't be dismissed or
assigned to the "do later" list. Without exception, you create your strongest, most telling energy through your beliefs
and thought patterns. All of your emotions are based in
your cognitions. Changing your thinking, then, isn't only
an energetic necessity, *it's your most empowering choice!* No
matter what you may have done to work on your goals in
the past, it is now time to start at the source. It's finally time
to take *complete control* of the powerful energy generator
that directs your destiny—your mind.

Our Mental Messes

Like Susan from the last chapter, very few people are really aware of how much garbage is cluttering up their thoughts and beliefs, especially concerning themselves. Some people just feel an undercurrent of discontent, while others live with chronic self-condemnation. For some, it's a subtle but nagging self-doubt, yet others are addicted to long lists of self-criticism, ready to judge themselves at the slightest provocation.

What about you? How often do you engage in self-judgment? Pay close attention to the way you talk to yourself, then ask yourself why. You may, in fact, be well intentioned about your self-judgment, thinking that it will actually help produce the results that you want. For example, you may think that judging yourself for being overweight will help motivate you to shed excess pounds. In reality, *judging yourself for anything will only attract someone who's equally willing to judge you*—not the outcome you were hoping for!

Self-acceptance doesn't mean that you have to approve of every little thing about yourself. When you drop the self-judgment, you can acknowledge the things you would like to change without the necessity of feeling ashamed.

This includes changing your energy. It's very important not to fault yourself for attracting what you have drawn to you in the past. This only sabotages your intention to attract something better. Beating yourself up for your old patterns only maintains them.

Negative self-talk isn't a form of facing up to some painful truth; in reality, the *truth* is very *rarely* revealed in your thinking. By releasing fear and self-criticism, you're actually awakening to your most fundamental truth—your value. In fact, embracing your value is the best way to foster the growth of love in your life.

No amount of self-criticism or self-judgment can be allowed to exist in an environment where the energy of love is being cultivated and nurtured. If you want to be loved, you must cut out the self-hate. Whether it's an obvious part of your nature or just an insidious, nearly subconscious pattern, you have to let it go. This must be a priority and an ongoing routine. Remember, the law is strict—the energy is absolute. If *you* can't engage in a different way of relating to yourself, then the way others relate to you will also never change.

Your self-perception *is* an energy, every bit as compelling as the energy of your aroma. You wouldn't walk around smelling like a garbage dump and still expect to attract the right person. Well, by the same token, you can't allow yourself to fill your mind and heart with the energy of stinking, self-critical garbage and still expect to attract the right person—or expect to receive the right treatment from the person you're with. It simply can't be done.

Mind Games

It's time to develop an awareness of exactly *what* you're thinking. Use your notebook again, and this time, instead of just counting them, *actually record the negative or self-critical thoughts that you find yourself thinking.* Go over the list of toxic thought patterns listed in the next section in order to identify the type of habit each statement represents.

After a few days, you'll find the same issues being repeated over and over again. You'll be surprised by how much your attitudes reflect the following patterns. Even if your negative assumptions aren't that numerous, jot every one of them down. This information will be the foundation for your future change, both in the energy of your thoughts and the emotions they create. Then the change in your destiny won't be far behind.

Here are the seven basic categories of negative thoughts or cognitions. How many of these do *you* engage in?

1. Devaluing

This is one of the two most common and destructive types of negative thought patterns. It's the practice of dismissing the value you could be finding—and acknowledging—in yourself, an experience, or another person. For example, the thought *I'm not good enough—I'm a loser* devalues yourself, while *They're such losers* devalues others.

People tend to depreciate their experiences all day long. If you're not doing something exciting, the weather isn't what you'd like, the task isn't "special," or the company not stimulating enough, then you see the experience as empty and valueless, even a burden. If you see *yourself* as not being "special" enough, then *you* will eventually feel valueless!

> *Devaluing is one of the surest ways to rob yourself of your potential for happiness. It creates a constant sense of bitterness, a nagging discontent about what's wrong with you and your life. This kind of energy can only magnetize more misery for you, so choosing to acknowledge the value—in yourself and your world— is your only option.*

Left unchecked, these habits of devaluing create very powerful emotions of hopelessness and depression. Such emotions project a heavy energy that's too thick to allow any light or vitality to penetrate it. The refusal to see value already present in your life will throw a wall up to block any more blessings from coming in.

If you feel chronic depression, you need to identify what you're devaluing—either in yourself or in your environment. You must continually shift your focus from what's wrong to what's right. If that which you focus on expands, do you really want your thoughts to be an endless litany of judgment and complaints?

It's time to embrace your real and eternal worth—you *are*

inestimably valuable as you are. No amount of judgment and striving will change that, and only the energy of total self-acceptance can stimulate acceptance from the outside world.

It's also time to start valuing your life. You may not be able to fill each day with stimulating people or provocative and challenging activities, but you *can* fill your perception with appreciation. You can have an attitude of gratitude! This requires a change in disposition, *an absolute refusal to minimize or devalue yourself or your life in any way*. When you make a determined choice to look for the good in your everyday experiences, value becomes your reality. And when value is what you live, value is what you attract!

2. Catastrophic Thinking

This is the other most common and destructive form of negative thinking. All of the other specific patterns of toxic thoughts fit into one of these two categories and should be approached with these issues in mind.

Catastrophic thinking is the practice of anticipating the worst possible outcome for a future activity or event. It can be as mundane as assuming "It's going to be a lousy day," or as significant as, "What if my marriage fails?" This form of thinking can take many forms, both verbal and visual, including the unbridled imaginings of future disasters.

I've had many clients vividly imagine everything from the betrayal of their spouses to the diagnosis of some exotic disease—even their own deaths. It's truly amazing how much of this fearful thinking we tend to engage in, always worrying about what horrible thing *could* go wrong.

This kind of worry—even if it's unspoken—carries with it an intense emotional consequence and a pervasive energy of fear. Fear is very agitating to your resonance, creating a repulsive charge. If fear is your dominant emotional energy, it will be impossible to relax. And without the peace of relaxation, there can be little positive attraction.

Being fearful about relationships can be their kiss of death. If you're afraid that you'll never attract a mate, you create a very desperate energy that reaches out in front of you and actually turns people away. If you're scared about maintaining your present relationship, you'll find yourself getting needy and clingy. This energy pushes your partner away, causing the very outcome you dread. Such fear sends very clear vibrational messages about your perception of yourself—you're energetically saying, "I'm not sure of my value as a partner." If you're not sure, who will be?

You must strike this and all worries from your cognitive repertoire. The only option is to choose trust instead of worry. "Brooding" and "what-if"-ing must be dispelled at every opportunity. Change your negative "what-if"s to positive ones, such as "What if it turns out great? What if my dreams *do* come true?"

You can't control the future, and no amount of worry in the present will create the energy you need to make it better. In fact, it's the energy of present worry that contaminates your future most. How can happy outcomes tune into your frequency when your mind is broadcasting wave after wave of pessimistic assumption?

3. Urgency

This form of negativity isn't limited to your thoughts—it can become an entire lifestyle. Urgent thinkers tend to make long lists of things to do, running all over the place, feeling they can't rest until everything is done. The problem is, there's always something new to add, the list never gets done, and the attitude creates a constant state of emotional and physical unrest, a truly upsetting energy that's bound to also send others running—in the opposite direction!

But urgency isn't just limited to the little activities of

daily life. It also applies to major issues, such as relationships and careers. Urgent thinkers have a great need to control other people and their environment. They tend to analyze everything that's going on around them in terms of how it will effect their own agenda. Much of their urgency comes from the need to be certain about how things will turn out. This turns into chronic analysis, scrutiny, and investigation, causing even more worry and urgency.

The resulting emotions create a cacophony of fragmented energy. Your focus is all over the place, usually *not* on what's going right. Perfectionism, control, fear, and lack are the resonance of the urgent heart, and this is a very agitated approach to life. Urgent thinkers are always hurried and worried—whether they're conducting important meetings or doing the most routine and mundane things, such as driving, housework, or even eating.

If you're an urgent thinker, you must ask yourself why you have to be so frantic about things. *Force yourself to slow down—both mentally and physically.* A leisurely pace creates a welcoming energy. Start to speak more calmly, drive more slowly, and eat more leisurely. Choose to *enjoy* the moment instead of racing through it.

Letting go of control and urgency will help manifest the vibration of peace and trust within and around you. This will make people much more receptive to you—and much more desirous of being in your company. The Universe loves a peaceful energy, and is much more willing to send wonderful outcomes to peace than to panic.

4. Comparing and Competing

In this modern, competitive world, it has become very common for people to compare themselves with others, usually in some negative way. They see people at work and think, *He makes more money than I do.* They see people on television and think, *She's so much prettier than I am.* This "win-lose mentality" makes life a neverending contest and a source of constant pressure. Everything, from competing in traffic to career promotions, becomes a measure of how well you're doing and what else you could do better. And when that's the case, everyone around you becomes a potential threat, a measure of how much you don't have— and perhaps will never get!

This kind of approach eats away at your joy for life. It becomes impossible to relax when you always feel like you're not measuring up. Loving yourself unconditionally is extremely difficult when you're always under pressure to do more, be more, and get what someone else has.

Life isn't fun when everything is a test. You can never really be happy when all you do is compete. And you can't help but project fearful, unloving energy when you feel defensive, threatened, or jealous. Feelings of jealousy splinter your harmonic connections with others. They make happiness a commodity that's conditionally meted out, instead of a state of mind that you consciously choose.

Real happiness comes from a self-acceptance that doesn't depend on measuring up to anyone else. *When you let go of the constant comparisons, you'll find that the world is a far less hostile place and that the Universe is far more responsive to your desires.* Instead of endless striving, you'll be able to take action with confidence and peace of mind, two essential elements in the achievement of your goals!

5. Victimization and Blame

Victimization thought-forms are usually born out of some trauma in the past, but they often globalize into the continued tendency to perceive yourself as being wronged by everyone. You blame others or your own history for the problems in your life, and consequently end up spending much of your time brooding about the past, complaining about the present, and making excuses for why things won't change in the future.

Many people actually like to remain victims because it makes them feel "special." Their pain gives them a unique kind of individuality, making them deserving of sympathy and concern, which can lend drama and even purpose to an otherwise lonely and seemingly meaningless life. It can even give some people a strange sense of misdirected power, using guilt or sympathy to manipulate others around them.

> *The victim mentality is totally disempowering. It works on the assumption that others are more capable of directing your life than you are. Such a disabling conclusion forces you to remain passive, convinced that you're defeated before you begin, blocking your positive energy and making it impossible to get anything wonderful back. Your insistence that* you have *been—or are being—victimized will only bring more evidence of that from the Universe.*

In this way, victimization and blame keep you stuck in a stagnant energetic pool. Your tendency is to lament your pain, focus on your rage, and live with chronic resentment. This is energetic paralysis! It can't possibly create any happiness in your life! Whether the offense happened long ago, or is an ongoing concern, your obsession about the offender constantly throws your power away. *You must get your power back!* Stop making other people responsible for your life. If you have unfinished anger, go ahead and get it out—write or talk about it, or get therapy if necessary. But you need to get it out *without letting it define you.* If it's a present concern, you'll absolutely need to deal with it. Feeling sorry for yourself only keeps you stuck.

It's time to move on. Instead of brooding, blaming, and making other people wrong, ask yourself, "What can I do *now* to take action in my own behalf?" Ask this often and when you get the answer, do it! Keep asking and keep doing! This way, you can begin to take responsibility for your present happiness *now*. It takes courage, but only *you* can make it happen. Energy begets energy. Happiness begets happiness. Responsibility gets the results.

6. Absolutes and All-or-Nothings

This type of thinking looks at things in the extreme, rarely considering the middle ground. Signal words are "always," "never," "everybody," "nobody," "too," "enough." The sentiments are often both devaluing and catastrophic— for example, "I'm too old to *ever* get married" or "I'll *always* have this weight problem" or "*Everybody* thinks I'm a jerk. *No one* will *ever* love me."

> *All-or-nothing statements are filled with fear and self-condemnation, which are the absolute worst things you can do to your energy! There's no room for self-condemnation in the effort to magnetize joy, and it should be avoided at all costs. Be vigilant about any fearful, self-critical thoughts. No matter what your reasoning for engaging in them, stop it—now! A truly attractive frequency never condemns itself!*

Whenever you catch yourself using all-or-nothing statements—even if only in your private thoughts—remember that they seriously darken your personal energy field. They project a self-aversion that can only cause aversion in others. No matter what you may have believed before, you aren't "too" anything—and you have "enough" of everything. The Universe accepts you as you are . . . it's time that you do, too.

If you use absolutes regarding the situations in your life, you could be setting yourself up for failure. Absolutes in the negative resound with expectations of lack. If you tell yourself such things as, "All the good ones are already taken," your belief will energize that into truth for you. The Universe is abundant and willing to provide you with your desires. But your beliefs are energetically stronger than your desires, and beliefs about absolute lack result in lack—absolutely.

"Always" and "never" are very long times. Strike the negative use of all of these signal words out of your vocabulary. Abundance is everywhere. *Anything is possible—at any time! Open yourself up to the options!*

7. Time Warping

This thought pattern is like catastrophic thinking, but includes the past as well as the future. Like victims, Time Warpers tend to rehash old experiences, but in this case they engage more in *self*-blame than blaming others. They relive old shame, replaying yesterday's conversations and reviewing last year's embarrassments. Their self-talk usually includes thoughts such as, *How could I have done that?* or *If only I'd said something different.*

If you find yourself brooding about the past, or if you have old shame that needs to be dealt with, it's time to forgive yourself. Write a compassionate letter to yourself—understand and affirm that you've always done the best that you could do given the circumstances you were in. Stop being your own judge and jury, condemning yourself to a life sentence of self-inflicted misery. No one is ruminating about your past as much as you are!

You *must* intervene on your need to judge old choices. As you let go, force yourself to focus only on the present. When that old sense of shame comes up, giving you that familiar pit in your stomach, take a deep breath, and as you exhale, affirm that you're releasing the past and any conclusions you may have made about it. Affirm, "I *deserve* to be forgiven; I *choose* to forgive myself now." Acknowledge that you can be truly free from the past by determining to truly *be* in the present.

In addition, be careful not to project your past problems onto future expectations. Time Warpers tend to repeatedly "run" anticipated events and potential encounters through their minds. They're often filled with dread about what to do and say, and they think this constant mental rehearsal will protect them in some way—perhaps even ensure a positive outcome. Unfortunately, this only makes them more anxious, sabotaging both their comfort in the present as well as their success in the future.

> *Focus only on the present! There are no solutions in the past and none in the future. You can't go back and redo it. You can't go ahead and control it. The only real solution is in the present, the only real control is in your thinking. The only way you can change the energy you attract later is to change the energy you create right now. In fact, the greatest power you can have over your future is the choice to empower yourself now.*

Moment and *momentum* have the same root word. *This is the moment that you create your energy momentum.* You can stay stuck in the past or you can take action in the present. Using the present to reverse these patterns is the most dynamic action you can take to direct your future destiny. Instead of lamenting who you were in the past, or worrying about who you will be in the future, *choose to accept who you are now,* no conditions, no exceptions! *Make* this *change in* this *moment, and you'll be guaranteed a dramatic change in your destiny!*

Everything that you do has an *immediate* energetic consequence, from your most monumental decision to your most subtle thought. In fact, the greatest consequences, for good or bad, are *always* the results of your thoughts.

So significant is the mind's impact on one's personal energy that no genuine pursuit of love or happiness can take place without investigating this connection.

Losing the "Loser" Mentality

Carol was a client who hadn't dated in several years. She was depressed and unhappy, and like so many women, attributed her unhappiness to the fact that she was alone. She assumed she was a "loser" because she hadn't been able to attract a guy. In fact, the reverse was true: The reason Carol hadn't been attracting a guy was *because she believed she was a loser.* Her personal energy field was full of self-condemnation and she magnetized the very same frequency from the men that she met.

Carol and I realized we would have to attack her toxic thinking in order to ch ange the negative energy she was putting out about herself. To do that, we used a process called "thought restructuring." This is a written exercise that uses the information about your thought patterns to *change* the underlying conclusions that are making you miserable and generating your negative energy.

You begin this process by first paying attention to your feelings. Feelings of discomfort are the "red flags" of your underlying negative thoughts and beliefs. Start by listing the *situations* that cause you to feel uncomfortable. Then list the *specific feelings* that you experience in each situation, such as anger, fear, anxiety, or depression. The following is an example taken from Carol's journal:

Situation	Feelings
Going to a party alone.	Embarrassed and depressed that I don't have a date. Nervous and uncomfortable talking to a new guy.

Once the specific feelings have been established, it's important to match them with the *thoughts* that are the source of those feelings. Ask yourself why you feel this way. What are you thinking? You may be able to find many of your answers in the statements from the list you made previously in your notebook. When you become aware of the thoughts behind your uncomfortable feelings, it's time to attack them.

Changing Your Mind

After you've isolated the stimulating situations and the emotions they evoke, you must then investigate your thought patterns. Divide your paper into two columns as shown in the example below. On the left side, place the negative thoughts, concerns, fears, and self-criticisms that arise in the situations you've described. Also identify the **toxic patterns** they represent:

1. Devaluing
2. Catastrophic thinking
3. Urgency
4. Comparing and competing
5. Victimization and blame
6. Absolutes and all-or-nothings
7. Time warping.

Place the appropriate pattern numbers next to each negative thought. Then on the right, *replace each thought with a different, more supportive and self-valuing option*. You don't have to be absolutely convinced of the optimistic conclusions at first, but you *must* write them down and be open to them as real options. In time, you'll be able to see their real truth and know that this is the *only healthy way* to think from now on. These thoughts are going to create the magnetism in your personal energy field, one that will bring you real happiness and will eventually attract the kind of love that you're looking for.

Following is a list of some of the thoughts that were at the basis of Carol's unhappiness, along with the responses that she chose to replace them. See if you can identify how your thinking might follow similar patterns. Using this as a sample, create your own thought restructuring sheet dealing with your own specific issues.

Thoughts and Concerns	Positive Options
What if people think I'm a loser because I'm alone? (Patterns 2 and 7)	It doesn't matter what people think. I'm *never* a loser. I'm whole and complete just as I am. *I* am all that I need. I'm great!
There must be something wrong with me if everyone else has a date. (Patterns 1 and 6)	I'm just as valuable and worthy as anyone else. I can believe in my value. I can relax, enjoy myself, and have fun.
What if he asks me out? I never know the right thing to say. (Patterns 2 and 6)	I'll be fine. I don't have to be perfect; I just have *to be myself and accept myself. I don't have to make it mean so much.*
What if he doesn't ask me out? I'm not good enough for him. He'll never find me attractive. I'm worthless. (Patterns 1, 2, 4, 6, and 7)	If he doesn't ask me out, it doesn't mean that I'm not attractive or not good enough. I will find the right person in the right time, and I will *always* value myself. I'm worthy and deserving. My life is of my own making.

Will the Person on the Right Please Stand Up?

The difference between the energies of each column is instantly apparent. First, go back and read *only* the column on the left. You'll clearly sense the energy of hopelessness and desperation that Carol was projecting. Then go back and read *only* the column on the right. You'll have an entirely different energetic reaction. Take a moment to do this now—it has a startling effect.

When Carol herself read the two columns separately, she was amazed at the difference in energy. She reflected, "Who would want to be with someone like the person on the left? Certainly not me!" Carol made an unwavering determination right then and there to become the "person on the right." She took the time to do this written thought restructuring process with *every* difficult situation, whether it concerned relationships or not. She identified *all* of her toxic patterns, uncovering the specific thoughts that led to her self-doubt and depression. She released those and continued making choices that provided her with healthier, more nurturing responses.

Carol especially recognized her tendency to make everything mean so much. She'd become addicted to "all-or-nothing" thinking, labeling every little experience as either the opportunity for total happiness or the potential for a lifetime of misery. Every man she met could be her ticket to heaven—yet, if he looked at her wrong, it sent her to hell. She had to learn to stop identifying the outside people and circumstances of her life as the source of all her problems and solutions. It was *she* who carried the *energy* of her problems and solutions within her. Her moment-to-moment attitudes created her resonance, the source of her happiness—as well as her misery.

Carol intervened on every old thought that projected a negative frequency and *inundated* herself with new, optimistic responses, until they were so familiar they actually became her spontaneous reaction. She took responsibility for her happiness and stopped looking to someone else for that.

It took a while, but in time, Carol noticed a big difference in how she was feeling. Her personal energy was changing. She felt lighter, more in control, and less like a victim. She was much happier, and she started attracting happier people and experiences to her.

Change Your Energy Now

Start doing your own thought restructuring sheets for every situation that you find uncomfortable. By doing this, you'll become aware of your most dominant and damaging thought patterns. Making new thought choices will help you release all of the potentially devaluing energies you're carrying in your personal energy field. *When you replace the weeds of self-criticism with the seeds of self-compassion, you'll be planting a garden of healthy, happy, and loving experiences to come.*

Every single time you change your thinking, you'll make a shift away from ugly, dark energies to brighter, more attractive ones. By changing the thoughts that you generate, you'll be changing your very life force, as well as changing *all of the consequences* that you set in motion for your future.

Like Carol, you can liberate yourself from that vague sense of hopelessness that's so devastatingly disempowering. When you do, your new sense of power and control will fill you with confidence and optimism—but you must keep at it. Like a dedicated gardener, you have to continue to weed out the old, destructive thoughts to keep them from coming back and choking out the new. Whenever you catch yourself catastrophizing about the future or devaluing yourself in any way, *you must force yourself to stop*—no matter how strong the compulsion to continue may be. No matter what, this is not an option! It's an absolute necessity. *You must stop polluting the energy you send out about yourself.*

Whenever provoked by uncomfortable emotions, try to

get at them and express the feelings. Then investigate the thoughts behind them by using this two column technique. Even if it's just at the end of the day, try to remember what you were thinking that may have made the experience so difficult. *Since it's not the situation but your perception of it that determines the energy you generate, you can choose to be completely in charge.*

Change your negative perception by replacing each thought with a more supportive, self-loving assertion. If you can't come up with a *positive* alternative to the toxic thought, *at least release the negative.* Say, "I don't have to think this way any longer" or "This thought doesn't serve me. I'm releasing it now" or "I can think better of myself, and as I let this thought go, I'm changing my energy and my future."

> *Everything you think moves outward from you in invisible—but unmistakable—waves of energetic information. If you believe you're a "loser," it will be very easy to attract losers and continually find yourself losing at love. If you believe you deserve the best, then the best is what you'll get. Remember this: The Universe always speaks your language.*

It's difficult enough to live in a world where criticism is so easily and indifferently extended by others. *Self-criticism* and *self-judgment* are *self-abuse.* By refusing to engage in the energy of self-abuse now, you'll stop the potential for abuse from others in the future. The Law of Magnetism will always respectfully send your own self-respect back to you. Since that self-respect is the most basic part of what you want to project, you shouldn't limit your thought restructuring sheets only to concerns and issues that have to do with romantic relationships. *Any* time you find yourself feeling bad about yourself, write down your thoughts, along with the corresponding healthy options.

Whether you realize it or not, your old fearful beliefs have always had a very real power over you. They dominate your energy with the momentum of repetition and emotional conviction. Unless you make a conscious and continuous choice to replace your negative thoughts with self-nurturing responses, the flow of toxic energy will persist in radiating out of your own heart center and will echo back to you from the hearts of those around you. Is this what you really want?

The Choice Is Always Yours

Thought restructuring will be a *vitally* important process if you intend to understand and change your energy dynamics. Your beliefs determine the very quality of your life experience, your tendency to be happy or unhappy. A heaviness of spirit creates a thick, dark density in your energy, a density that will return in your destiny!

It's time to lighten up, to brighten your energy by letting go of your dark thoughts. But changing your thoughts isn't just some mindless busywork, designed to create a Pollyanna-like attitude. It's the alternator that can bring a positive and powerful charge to your personal energy field. Quantum physics shows that consciousness creates reality, and *your* consciousness has the power to create *your* reality. That reality can either be bogged down by suffering or be blessed by all of the magic and joy that the Universe has to offer.

The choice is yours. You don't have to continue projecting your old energy, sending out wave after wave of negative frequency. You can begin now to alternate your current to a more positive attitude. When you choose optimistic instead of pessimistic responses to the situations of your life, you'll be able to make quantum leaps in the direction of manifesting all that you desire.

❧ Chapter Five ❧

Your Affirmative Action

"There is nothing either good or bad,
but thinking makes it so."
— William Shakespeare

The energy of love resonates most strongly to the vibration of affirmation. Throughout the Universe, all of life affirms itself in sound, movement, and power. In the ever-present light and heat of the sun, in the lion's roar or the kitten's purr, in the deafening percussion of great waterfalls or the quiet awakening of movement at sunrise, nature is constantly affirming its vitality and value. We, too, contribute to this Universal symphony in every life-honoring sound, thought, or choice that we make.

The intention to affirm is the intention to love *that which you're affirming.* To be affirmative is to recognize worth; to acknowledge and appreciate; and to be focused on value. The more positive your intention, the more you'll magnetize validation and love from the Universe. For this reason, the conscious practice of affirmation is one of the most dynamic ways you can change your personal reality.

As a tool, affirmation is relatively simple: *It's the repetition of a nurturing and optimistic conclusion with the intention to be open to its truth.* With this as its basic format, affirmation can be used to deal with virtually any issue, problem, or desire—producing results so amazing you may have never even thought them possible. For instance, a friend of mine wanted to purchase a new home that was way out of his range financially. Yet every night before sleep, he affirmed that the money he needed was coming to him. Within four months he had the down payment for the house and was signing the purchase agreement.

Author and lecturer Laura Silva tells the story of a woman who wanted to lose weight. Every morning in the shower, this woman affirmed that the water was washing her fat away—in six months, she lost 30 pounds, claiming she didn't consciously change her lifestyle to any great degree.

A client of mine combined relaxation with affirmation to heal a bleeding ulcer. Another used *affirmation saturation,* which is the relentless repetition of very specific affirmations, to break the grip of a paralyzing anxiety condition. Still another used affirmation to quit cigarettes after a lifetime of smoking two packs a day.

In spite of such remarkable results, affirmation is often dismissed as being too simplistic and unrealistic; therefore, it's considered to be ineffective. But in order to understand how truly dynamic affirmative self-talk can be, it's necessary to look at how our brains work in determining our positive or negative reactions.

Driving the Mind

Where does your mind go when you're not driving it? It's always in gear, so it's always heading somewhere. Whether you're consciously directing it or not, it's always on the road to creating your life energy. Isn't it time to get in the driver's seat and actively determine your mind's destination?

Every time you have a thought, a series of neurons are fired, triggering tiny electrical impulses. All of your cognitive responses follow neural pathways in your brain. Based mostly on your repeated experiences and what you've learned, your thought responses will follow the same pathways when exposed to the same types of stimulation. For example, if some childhood trauma taught you to be afraid of dogs, then anytime you're exposed to a dog, your brain will respond with the same impulses and negative, fearful assumptions. It's immediate and automatic—the more emotionally charged the issue, the more certain and swift the response.

Unfortunately, these imbedded patterns can't be erased. They don't just go away once you decide you no longer want to react that way. The only way to change these responses is to *build other patterns of neural pathways*. To do this, two things must happen: First, you must learn to be more relaxed, both in life in general, and in the stimulating situations. Then you must *consciously and consistently choose different conclusions* about your experiences. With enough repetition, this action creates new patterns of neural pathways that eventually lead to different thoughts. Without this process, the brain simply does not know that it has any other options.

It's like driving to work—after years of taking the same route every day, it becomes a spontaneous activity that you don't even think about. You just do it, often arriving without any conscious memory of the process of getting there. This is what happens with your negative thinking—your thoughts follow the same old pathways. You don't even have to think about how you arrive at the conclusions—they're just your spontaneous reactions.

Let's say, though, that after years of taking the same route to work, someone tells you about a shortcut. At first, you even forget to take the shortcut, since you're so accustomed to the old route. When you do remember, however, the streets are strange and unfamiliar to you. It takes some conscious thought to change your habit, but you're willing to do it because it helps in the long run. In time, you start to become accustomed to the new way, and you feel more comfortable. Eventually, with enough repetition, the new route becomes as spontaneous as the previous one.

Retraining your neural pathways is a similar, but much more profound, process. You *must* give yourself options. You must see the options as logical and beneficial to you. And you must be unceasing in your willingness to repeat the options until they, too, develop a spontaneity of their own.

The pattern of responding negatively—even when you don't want to—has been called *neural hijacking.* This is the kind of uncontrollable and immediate power the brain has in predetermining your responses. If you don't want to be "hijacked" into negativity anymore, you have no choice but to decide consciously that you'll only allow nurturing and optimistic responses to dominate your brain's activities.

The stronger and more emotional your old responses are, the more deeply imprinted the neural pathways will be. This will make it all the more necessary to persist with the repetitions of the healthy new beliefs and affirmations. No matter how compelled you may be to engage in the old thoughts, you must be willing to continue the process of consciously changing your beliefs until you actually *feel* yourself becoming more hopeful, positive, and optimistic.

Whether you realize it or not, you've already made some very important conclusions about yourself and your life. Some of the most common toxic conclusions I hear are: *It matters what people think. I have to live according to other people's expectations. I need a relationship to be happy. I don't measure up to most people. I have to be thin to be beautiful. I have to follow my partner's agenda or the relationship won't last.* Do you recognize any of these? There are plenty more where they came from.

The word conclusion *means thought or opinion;
it also means the final outcome of something, the way
something ends. Be assured, there's a direct connection
between your mental conclusions and the final results
of your sought-after goals. It's a very real energetic
vibration of cause and effect. The conclusions of your
mind—good or bad—will actually lead to the conclusions of your dreams.*

Have you ever seen a drawing of a lightbulb over a car-
toon character's head, or heard the phrase "lightbulb
moment" to represent a brilliant idea or profound realization? Whoever created this metaphor had no idea how
accurate it was. The fact is, if all of the neurons of your brain
were to fire at once, it would actually produce enough electricity to illuminate a lightbulb—such is the power of your
mind, and the electromagnetic power of your thoughts!
This is why the thought-restructuring process is so important. It reveals the old unwanted conclusions, and creates
much healthier and more desirable options. But bringing
these new, healthy beliefs into your daily consciousness
and your personal energy field will require more than that—
it will require the process of *repeated affirmation,* an affirmative intention that never stops.

Once Is Not Enough

Affirmation saturation is an aggressive approach
designed to deal with especially difficult problems and stub-
born thought patterns. You begin by choosing (or creating)
50 to 100 affirmations that address your own needs, then you
repeat them at least 5 to 10 times per day, until you feel your
mood begin to change.

To determine what issues you need to address in your
affirmations, look back to your thought-restructuring sheets.

The optional replacement thoughts from the right-hand column will provide you with your own tailor-made affirmative statements. Write these out on a separate sheet of paper, and in addition to these, add a number of affirmations about self-valuing and self-empowerment. If you need to, you can even affirm that you have the strength and discipline it takes to do this process! Compile at least 50 affirmations of this type all in one place. (I put my affirmations on index cards, which I keep in various places, such as my purse or the nightstand next to my bed.)

You must then repeat this entire set of affirmations many times a day, *perhaps even every hour.* You want to try to get *at least* five repetitions of 50 affirmations each day. The format that produces the most spectacular results, however, calls for ten repetitions of 100 affirmations each day. At first this seems like a daunting task, but if you force yourself to take the action, you'll be truly amazed by the results.

I've had many clients who have called me within the first week of starting this process. They report being able to do things they've never done before, with more comfort than they ever thought possible. When they truly inundate themselves with positive perceptions, they consistently find themselves feeling stronger, more relaxed and creative— even more attractive. And they're often surprised by how many little "magical" things begin to happen in their lives.

If 500 to 1,000 affirmations a day seems extreme, and you don't want to put this kind of effort into dealing with your negative perceptions; you must realize that *you'll end up putting even more effort into constantly dealing with the pain and problems that your negative energy keeps bringing to your life.* If you're truly willing to "do whatever it takes" to turn your life around, then you should be willing to do this. It *will* pay off!

Fear and negativity are dominant forces in modern society. A peaceful and affirmative heart shines like a lighthouse in the darkness, illuminating and attracting all around it. You can choose to hold on to your negative thoughts and remain in the darkness—or you can make affirmation the radiant center of your life, and you can become a beacon of joy and a focal point for returning love.

Your Affirm-Options

The ideal way to create your own affirmations is to identify the specifics of your negative self-talk and then counteract those negative beliefs with positive, healthy responses. (For wording, use the seven tips described below.) At first it may be difficult to say statements that seem to contradict the fundamental beliefs that you've been embracing for years. Long-held beliefs, even the most destructive ones, often seem to have the ring of truth to them. And if your parents are the source of those beliefs, there's often an especially compelling attachment that may be very difficult to fight. By choosing new beliefs, you may feel as if you're lying to yourself, denying reality, or even possibly betraying your parents.

But it's time to create your own reality. It's time to determine *for yourself* the kind of energy you want to attract to your life. You have every right—in fact, every reason and responsibility—to consciously determine the nature of *your own thoughts*. Remember that *no matter what you've been told in the past, or have been taught to believe about yourself or the world, you do have the option and the power to change it.* You can choose to embrace a different, more affirmative attitude *at every opportunity* from now on. It's your option—and your energetic necessity.

Danny's Notebook

I once had a client named Danny, who was a soft-spoken man in his late 30s. He'd suffered from a condition called social anxiety disorder all of his life. Even when he was very young, he was painfully shy and afraid around other people. But in spite of all of that, he made his way through school, graduated from college, and got a job. But Danny's romantic life left a lot to be desired. In fact, except for a very few short-term, uncomfortable relationships in college, Danny had hardly dated at all.

When he came to me, he wanted to achieve two things: first, to learn to be more comfortable in all kinds of social situations; then to be able to attract and maintain a healthy romantic relationship. This was a big task, but I knew he could do it.

As with all social anxiety conditions, Danny had developed an obsessive concern about what people think. He'd always felt somewhat inadequate, so he was always looking for people's approval. Trying to anticipate what people expected, and consequently feeling nervous about living up to those imagined expectations, was the source of his anxiety. This unending effort of anticipating and performing made it impossible for Danny to be comfortable in public. And, of course, his anxiety only got worse when he was in the presence of women.

We examined Danny's beliefs. He knew he had to make his self-acceptance far more important than acceptance from others. It was hard, but he needed to arrive at the conclusion that it just didn't matter what anyone—even women—thought.

After dozens of thought-restructuring sheets, he began to consolidate his healthy, affirmative responses in a pocket-sized notebook. Eventually this little red notebook was filled with affirmations about his value, peace of mind, and ability to be and accept himself. Danny kept his little notebook in his shirt pocket all of the time. Many times throughout the day, he'd flip it open and read whatever affirmations were on that page. He also read them every morning upon waking, and every evening before bed.

I remember that notebook well. Danny used it and used it, and its little red cover got so beat up, it had to be held together with tape—but that notebook meant everything to Danny. The conclusions in it represented a new life for him. It reminded him of the control he now took over his thinking and the power he now had to change his destiny. And, in time, that notebook became Danny's key to breaking out of the limiting beliefs that had kept him imprisoned his entire life.

Ultimately, Danny was able to change his perception of himself. He no longer cared what people thought. It took a while, but the thoughts in the notebook had become real and spontaneous. He took those new thoughts into social situations—into every situation—and made them his reality. And, of course, his reality subsequently changed.

I ran into Danny about a year after we stopped working together. I noticed that the ever-present notebook wasn't in his shirt pocket where it had always been. (From the very beginning he had liked the idea of keeping his new beliefs close to his heart.)

When I asked him where the notebook was, he laughed. "I don't need it *over* my heart," he said, "when I've got it *in* my heart."

Danny told me that he no longer felt any anxiety when he was out in public. In fact, he said he couldn't even remember why he'd ever felt so afraid. Then he pulled out his wallet . . . and asked if I wanted to see a picture of his wife. I was ecstatic for Danny, for he had achieved his goals. He was comfortable in public and found the love he was looking for. Although he used a lot of techniques—such as relaxation—in addition to the affirmations, he attributes the turning point of his recovery to his relentless pursuit of a new system of beliefs.

Wouldn't it be worth it to create your own life-changing notebook? Use it to help you *choose your conclusions with intention and clarity.* Fill it with statements charged with emotions of optimism and determination. As you create these new statements, remember that what you're creating is your energetic destiny.

Until you can come up with a list of affirmations designed specifically for your own needs, here are some that can help you create new patterns of neural responses and self-accepting energy. We start with self-valuing, because that's the energy that will bring appreciation from others and desirable experiences into your life.

Write down the statements that are most appropriate for you. Carry them with you, and read them *several times a day*. Remember that repetition and conviction are the only ways to create new habits strong enough to change the old patterns. And since every thought carries an energetic consequence, *these* are definitely the thoughts you want to make real.

Affirmations for Self-Valuing

- *I always deserve to love and respect myself.*

- *I deserve to be loved and respected by others.*

- *No matter what I may have believed in the past, I now embrace myself as a worthy and valuable person.*

- *There is abundant love and wealth in the Universe, and I am worthy of receiving all that I desire. I'm attracting that love and wealth now.*

- *Every day, I affirm and acknowledge my worth and my value.*

- *I'm learning to intervene on any statement of self-criticism.*

- *I create wonderful, self-affirming energy in my thinking.*

- *I'm strong. I'm determined. I'm capable of creating my destiny now.*

- *The quality (and energy) of my life is up to me, determined by the thoughts that I choose to think and the choices I choose to make.*

- *The quality (and energy) of my relationships is up to me, determined by the ways that I treat myself and talk to myself every day.*

- *I believe in myself; I accept myself. I'm magnetizing others who accept and believe in me also.*

- *I'm learning to accept and love everything about myself. I'm valuable!*

- *I never minimize myself in any way. I deserve my own love.*

- *I have all that I need to create the energy that will magnetize great things. I know that now.*

- *I choose to believe only the best about myself. It is my truth.*

- *I deserve to be happy. I choose to be happy. Happiness is becoming a way of life for me.*

- *The more I create value in my thinking, the more I create happiness in my life.*

- *I release all self-criticism. It's just an old habit. I embrace myself with love.*

- *I choose to be optimistic about myself and my life now.*

- *From now on, all that I say, think, and do will be devoted to promoting the energy of love within myself and within my life. It's my energetic choice.*

These are just some examples of the new ways you can *choose* to think. Look at them as your new reality, not just some silly busy work. It's a simple formula, but a *very* powerful one. Just as the quantity and types of food that you eat will determine your physical health and even your looks; the quantity and quality of the thoughts that you think will determine your emotional health and your energetic attraction. You can't consume a diet of negative thoughts and then look in the mirror of your life and be surprised when you see negativity staring back at you!

Pollyanna Had a Point!

There's a wonderful story about a little girl whose refusal to think anything negative changed an entire town. In this story, Pollyanna encourages people to stop seeing themselves as sick, alone or hopeless in any way. Even when things are hard, she teaches them to play the "glad game," a game where the person tries to find at least one thing to be glad about, no matter what difficulty they may be experiencing.

This inspiring story was very popular several years ago. Over time, however, people have begun to see themselves as too sophisticated to engage in such a simplistic approach to things. In fact, the name *Pollyanna* is now often used as a term of derision, a way to belittle someone who is "too optimistic," implying that they're not being realistic enough.

But Pollyanna had a point! As simplistic as it might sound, there's no reason to *ever* engage in pessimism. No matter what difficult experience you're faced with, pessimism does not help the situation. It doesn't change things for the better. It doesn't empower you or anyone involved. And it certainly doesn't create the kind of energetic environment that fosters miraculous and happy outcomes.

In fact, no matter what the obstacle, it's utterly self-defeating to engage in the energy of pessimism, precisely at the time you need a miracle most!

Only the energy of optimism and value can create the miracle you need at *any* given moment. You must assume the best, and you must search for something to value in your life, no matter what hardship you may be enduring. The "glad game" is a way to find something of value, something that could be appreciated no matter what else is going on. This is a powerful decision at any time, for *the choice to appreciate and acknowledge value always attracts more value*. Of course, Pollyanna had no awareness of quantum physics. She just knew it made her feel better, and when she taught it to others, it made them feel better, too. Pessimism, on the other hand, only succeeds in making people feel worse.

Because optimism is emotionally beneficial, it's also energetically favorable. Emotions charge your energy, and the excitement that comes from optimism pumps up the volume of your magnetic resonance more than almost any other emotion. So whether you decide to be optimistic because it makes you feel better, or because you finally realize that it's necessary to change your energy, it doesn't really matter. The magnetic consequences of your optimism will remain the same. When you choose to be optimistic, you radically change your electromagnetic field, bringing a brighter, happier light frequency to your world—and to the world of those around you.

For this reason, the importance of the daily practice of affirmative self-talk cannot be overemphasized. People often feel silly when they start this process, but *don't let this stop you*. Say them in the shower, in your car, cleaning the house, and *every time you look into the mirror*. You must *inundate* yourself with healthy, compassionate and encouraging self-talk every day.

Change Your Energy Now

It's time to change your life from negation to affirmation: Create your own affirmative intentions; be as positive and as self-nurturing as possible; fill your heart and saturate your consciousness with these new ideas.

Here are some tips for creating powerful personal affirmations:

1. Never phrase affirmations in terms of what you *don't* want. (For example, instead of "I'm not going to attract hurtful men anymore," use "I'm attracting healthy, loving, and supportive men.")

2. Always make the affirmation about yourself, not about other people. (For example, instead of, "He's becoming more and more attracted to me," use, "I'm becoming more and more attractive every day.")

3. If it's hard to verbalize a strongly positive statement with conviction, such as, "I totally accept myself as I am," you can soften it by adding phrases like, "beginning to" or "learning to." (For example, "I'm *learning to* accept myself as I am.") These statements might be easier to say at first, and easier for the subconscious mind to accept. In time, however, you should move on to the more absolute statements of total self-love and self-acceptance, for these more aptly represent your true personal reality—as well as your preferred energy.

4. Make some affirmations in the second person. Say these while looking in the mirror. (For example, in addition to, "I'm valuable and

deserving of love," look at yourself in the mirror and say, "You're valuable and deserving of love.") This is very important. Don't skip this step, thinking it's silly or unproductive.

5. Use the present tense, even when describing an event that hasn't yet manifested in the physical realm. (For example, instead of, "I'll have a happy romance in my life," use, "I have a happy romance in my life. I have a great romance.")

6. Add some emotional energy to your affirmations. (For example, "I'm *excited* about the love in my life," and, "I'm *thrilled* about the happy romance I have in my life.")

7. Say your affirmations out loud, as it amplifies the energy of your intentions. Speak them with conviction, and be open to hearing their truth.

It's true that our society and training can make it difficult to be affirmative and optimistic 100 percent of the time. Don't worry—if you judge yourself for your negative thoughts, you're only adding negation to negation. You must forgive yourself and move on. Let yourself experience and express your honest feelings, and then release them. Rededicate yourself to focusing on the pluses, and the pluses will multiply.

Your personal energy field resonates with both your affirmative and negative energy. When you understand that your whole life is based on the exchange of this energy, you will realize how vitally important affirmation is. Whether spoken or just thought, there are always energetic consequences to your conclusions.

*Which would you rather experience—the consequences
of the positive or the negative energy of your thoughts?
You create them both.*

Keep in mind that old definition of insanity: Doing the
same old things in the same old ways and expecting different results. If you hope to make the desired changes in your
life, you *must* start *doing* and *thinking* things differently
now—it's the only way to generate a new magnetic energy.
Without this change in your mental focus, you'll be *guaranteed* the same results. The price you must pay is your willingness to *change your thinking*. The prize is your happiness—
in life and in love.

❧ CHAPTER SIX ❧

The Heart of the Matter

*"God is love; and he that dwells in love
dwells in God, and God in him."*
— 1 John 4:16

There's one more very important component to the light energy we project: It's not just determined by how we mentally *perceive* ourselves, it's also determined by how we *experience* ourselves. For the most part, our day-to-day experience of ourselves is based on the physical and emotional sensations of our lives, which is often colored by our *perceived* limitations and weaknesses. But there's a part of our nature that's never weak. It has never been limited, and is totally free of all vulnerability. This is our spiritual self, our true and essential self—our soul.

The soul is never detached from us, but the chaos of everyday life often results in a very strong sense of separation. In fact, it's this sense of disconnection, the chronic feeling that something is missing, that makes us yearn for love even more fiercely. The feelings of loss, the need and longing that keep tugging at our hearts, are born out of a distant but nagging memory of our most powerful love experience.

For whether we know it or not, what we're longing for is the once-familiar love of God. This love has always been—and continues to be—freely given. And, although it may seem merely a distant dream, it continues to be thoroughly experienced by our spirit, our higher self. Unfortunately, our personal selves remain out of touch with this love, largely *because we're constantly distracted by our efforts to replace it!*

In order to reexperience the extent of God's love in our life and to see the source of our truest value and most authentic power, it's necessary to reconnect with our long-missed—and perhaps long-forgotten—spiritual nature. This is the part of our self that lives with God's presence in every moment, the part of our being that's still completely within us and yet moves freely through the Universe, helping us pursue that which we most deeply desire. This fully loved, freely moving, and always present part of ourselves is our soul, a vital part of our identity that's ignored by so many!

The experience of our soul opens us up to all possibilities. It creates a reverence of self and life that radiates a brilliant vibration. Our soul is connected with the Divine, and our awareness of it allows us to feel the worthiness of Divine love in our own eternal heart. When we can finally feel that worthiness, it becomes impossible not to project it to the world!

The Sound of the Soul

There are many things that can help you come in contact with your soul, such as art, dance, music, love, appreciation, prayer, and compassion. But there's one thing that you need to do on a daily basis if you wish to discover the profound inner knowing of your soul's presence. This is the pursuit of the silent mind—the practice of meditation.

Silence and nonactivity are necessary because the daily

confusion of life magnifies that sense of separation between your physical reality and your spiritual power. Therefore, the foundation of most types of meditation requires a silent environment, a quiet and relaxed body, and a still mind. The goal is to shut out both the external and the internal noises that distract you from that peaceful presence within.

Some forms of meditation repeat a word or a phrase, called a "mantra." Others revolve around a process of regular breathing, mentally following each breath in and out in a regular, methodical pattern. Still others encourage you to focus on your heart area, visually bathing it in a healing light. In time, this heart-centered focus should lead you to a deepened awareness of your very real and eternal self.

When you meditate regularly, you'll feel both a depth and an expansiveness that's far more profound than even the fullest extent of your physical experience. You'll begin to identify something that is all you—and yet much more of you than you'd previously imagined.

With continued meditation, feelings of peacefulness, joy, and strength will begin to permeate all the areas of your life. You'll feel a lightening of spirit, a tranquility of being right down to your cells. Internal conflict begins to subside, and external conflict is much easier to transcend.

The Bridge to Everywhere

The daily practice of meditation will open you up to amazing experiences and information. You'll begin to receive intuitive messages, guidance, and subtle suggestions from a side of you that has access to all of the wisdom and knowledge that you will ever need. This is your higher self.

I use the term "higher self" to indicate the consciousness of your soul. But "higher" doesn't mean above or better than you. This actually promotes the sense of separation that we're so desperately trying to resolve! Yes, the soul is larger than the body. Its presence is everywhere. But its power isn't only *outside* of you. Although your soul's consciousness reaches to the ends of existence, it's also *within* every cell of your being. Higher doesn't mean separate and outside; it means expressing at a higher frequency or vibration.

Your higher self vibrates with the wisdom and consciousness of your soul. It remembers its source, its past and future. Your higher self knows more about you than you consciously know about yourself. It knows where you need to go and what you need to decide. Because your soul remembers, it has far more answers than your logical mind can provide on its own. And it's always available to you, communing with you, day and night, hour upon hour, through good times or bad.

Your soul also has access to all of the feelings and qualities that you seek, even if you've never encountered them in your personal life. Even if you feel you've never been loved, your soul has been. It knows with certainty what it feels like to be loved absolutely. You may have never felt lovable, but your soul knows the beauty and loveliness of your heart, and it can show you how truly lovable you are. You may think you've never felt strong, confident, or courageous, but your soul has experienced all these things for you and is waiting to bring these qualities to your personal life.

You can use this fascinating power of your soul's knowing to create the compelling confidence and self-valuing that will draw real love into your life. Whenever you need to feel a certain kind of strength—whether it be grace, courage, dignity, perseverance, patience, trust, love, or any other quality you may feel that your personal self may be lacking—you can draw it up from your soul's experience. Here's how:

First, meditate on your heart center. From that heart center, visualize the glowing light of your higher self. Within that light, you can feel the pulsating presence of the quality that you're looking for. Name that specific quality. Is it the confidence to go after your dreams? The courage to confront a problem? The discipline to stop an addictive behavior? No matter what it is, your soul can produce it for you whenever you call upon it to do so. Know that it's there!

As you visualize the energy of that specific quality throbbing within your heart center, imagine what it would *feel* like. Allow its energy to grow stronger and brighter in your heart. Feel the light of this quality filling your body, your mind, and your own energy. Feel it empowering you, radiating through you, giving you a sense of complete assuredness, peace, and strength.

You can rely on the energy of any quality being there whenever you need it, and you can access it anytime you desire—all you have to do is name it and know that it is there. Close your eyes, breathe deeply into your heart center, and allow yourself to feel its power growing within you and giving you its strength.

The more you practice this meditation, the easier it will be to tap into the energy that any situation requires. Imagine how very empowering it would be to be able to access whatever emotional state or strength of character that you may ever need. Sound impossible? It's not! With enough practice, you'll be able to call upon any life-enhancing energy and quickly feel that force guiding your heart.

The Grand Relationship

Meditation is one of the strongest conduits to the ultimate power in the Universe—the Divine presence within you. It brings you a firm but peaceful sense of your power, one that's based on the deepest, most profound part of your nature—that is, your loving connection with God. In fact, the most important reason for meditation is that it connects you directly with the source of Universal love. It allows you to *actually experience* the utterly sublime affection and acceptance from your most important loving partner, your Divine partner.

Some people might ask what relationships have to do with God. But to me, this one connection sets the stage for all others. Writing a book about relationships without talking about God would be like writing a book about anatomy without talking about the heart!

Perhaps the concept of God as an ever-present source of love is foreign to you. Perhaps what you've been taught to believe about God has been negative or frightening. Many people even have trouble saying the word *God*. Their history has formed a perception of God that generates fear and dread. If this is the case with you, it is now time to look into your soul and remember the truth.

> *Allow yourself to see the Divine power of the Universe as loving, creative, willing, and supportive. Whether you call this loving spirit God, the Universe, Eternal Wisdom, Loving Source, or anything else, know that in the center of your being is the essence of your deepest identity, your favorite friend, your most caring parent, your dearest and sweetest love.*

God, this Universal Consciousness, is with you and in you. Your relationship exists, even if you don't know it or would prefer to deny it. It's there to bring great things into your life. But—like all relationships—you must take an active part. You can do this through meditation, and it's well worth the time and energy. When you make God your partner, you'll be connecting with your closest confidant, your greatest support, your most passionate and enduring love!

In reality, God *is* your most important ally, the Grand Relationship of your life, the source of all comfort and complete acceptance, the very origin of the love you're seeking. Developing a personal connection with the Divine in your life will help you to finally realize the true extent of your authentic power and eternal value. Only then will you finally be able to stop the external seeking and striving, and arrive at an inner peace that's so profound, it will change how you feel about everything.

You're never alone when you're with the Divine—*and you are always with the Divine.* You're never weak, vulnerable, or unwise, for in the presence of the Divine, there's nothing to fear and nothing to need! God is complete, and so are you in His presence. From your eternal origin, you've always been complete. This is the blessing of God's *love.* It's extended outward to you in any condition, under any circumstance, within any situation. *There's nothing you can do to make God love you more—and nothing you can ever do will cause God to love you less.*

Actively feeling God's unwavering love *constantly* confirms your worthiness. It creates within you a real reverence for yourself and your life, one that resonates outward from you in a sparkling vortex of love. Your personal energy field radiates with brilliant beauty, dignity, and joy.

In fact, your soul is where *real* beauty is born. People think that beauty is a physical quality. It isn't. It is, first and foremost, energetic. Whether or not people are attracted to you will depend much more upon the beauty of your soul than on any aspect of your outward appearance.

For instance, we all know people who might not be considered physically beautiful, yet their energy is enormously appealing. Their inner loveliness brings them truly loving relationships, many friends, fulfillment, and even wealth. Yet we also know people who would be considered by most to be physically attractive, even stunning, but for some unknown reason, they have few friends, no romantic relationships, and a lot of frustration in their lives. They appear to be attractive, but they can't attract. The sad reality is that in most of these cases, the person's heart is so heavily laden with fear and negativity that they totally cut themselves off from the beauty, power, and love of their soul. This creates an ugly energy that's strong enough to cast a pall on even the most striking physical appearance.

So if it's *real* beauty you're looking for, you need to be more conscious of your soul than you are of your hair, body, clothes, or makeup. Your soul is already perfectly beautiful, and meditation will help you to see that beauty and express it to others. It's the beauty regimen of the heart, and you need to make it a part of your daily life.

Your Magnetic Light

One process of meditation that I teach my clients is a guided visualization to enhance attraction. You can do it when you go to bed, or anytime that you're able to physically relax without distractions.

> *Picture your heart as a great source of power, sending a bright and radiant light far out into the Universe. Know that this light is the energetic radiance of your higher self, and fill its brilliant rays with the energy of self-love, confidence, courage, and real beauty. Feel it pulsating with the magnetism of a strong, self-affirmed spirit. See your spirit-light radiating outward with confidence and self-love—feel the sense of joy and expectation it creates.*
>
> *You begin to notice other lights gravitating toward your light out in the distance. Some are the soul-lights of people you already know, who are willing to respond more compassionately, bringing more peace and joy into your life. Others are the lights of new friends, being drawn to you in loving interest and timeless recognition.*
>
> *Watch this attraction grow stronger as your energy draws these lights to you. If you're looking for a romantic relationship, affirm that one of these lights is your ideal partner who's bringing a wonderful, mutually nurturing relationship to you. Know that it is so.*

As you fall asleep or conclude the meditation, release the images with trust. Send your soul-light out into the Universe with the certain knowledge that it moves before you in time and space, planting the seeds of magnetic attraction in situations you have yet to experience.

This meditation, along with the regular practice of a quiet mind, can lay the groundwork for some very power-ful energetic changes. But this *must* be backed up with an unwavering determination to bring the light of self-valuing into your life. Like the light of your higher self, your thoughts must vibrate with self-love, and your choices must pulsate with honor.

❦ CHAPTER SEVEN ❧

The Power of Your Choices

*"Our free and undetermined moral choices and the
worlds they coauthor are like an electron's virtual
transitions. They are experiments in reality creation."*
— Danah Zohar

Every day you make choices that either enhance your
energy of honor or deplete it. From deciding what
and how much to eat, to choosing how you talk to
yourself and others, your life is filled with unending
options that energetically lead you in one direction or
another.

Your honor and dignity are two of your most valuable
commodities. Losing either could be the single most damaging influence on your personal energy field. When a
relationship demands that you sacrifice these things, even
to a small degree, you lose a part of yourself. If enough
honor or dignity is lost, you'll eventually lose your self-
respect, as well as the respect of your partner. The resulting
relationship turns into one of emptiness—with a nagging
sensation of self-betrayal.

A Matter of Honor

Compromising your honor can happen in great or small ways, but even seemingly minor compromises will eventually lead to resentment and dissatisfaction. Here's an example.

A client of mine named Lauren started dating someone new. After a few weeks, he explained to her that he was having some problems with his business, so they started going "dutch"—each paying for his or her share of meals and entertainment. Lauren was very sympathetic that her guy was having financial difficulties, so she soon began to pay for his expenses as well as hers. At first, this was an easy thing for her to do; in time, however, she noticed that he was spending more money on personal things for himself while he was still allowing her to pay for both of them on their dates. She wanted to say something, but since she found him desirable in every other way, she held her tongue. Lauren was afraid she'd lose him if she confronted him. As it became more and more apparent that his business problems were turning around, though, she felt her resentment building.

The holidays came around about nine months into the relationship, and Lauren was convinced that her boyfriend would show his appreciation for her at this time. But he didn't. All he gave her was some excuse about year-end taxes—which she tried to understand. She didn't want to be petty, and she certainly didn't want to end her relationship over "material things," so she remained silent.

He slowly started becoming stingy with other things, like his affection and time. When Lauren's birthday arrived in January, her boyfriend was out of town. He called to wish her a happy birthday, but that was the only way he acknowledged Lauren's special day. And in February, when Valentine's Day was coming up (along with the year's anniversary of their first date), Lauren suggested a special celebration. The reaction she got depressed her, but came as no surprise: He gave her countless reasons why it couldn't happen, including not enough time and not enough money.

Lauren felt deflated. She walked away from that conversation wanting to cry, feeling as if she "had a big, aching hole" in her chest. She felt minimized, discounted, and confused—and hopeless about continuing the relationship.

In our session following this episode, I asked Lauren if continuing to see this guy would be honoring to her—would it promote her sense of dignity? I'd asked her this many times in the past, and at those times she'd always reacted defensively, going into long rationalizations of her boyfriend's behavior. But this time the answer was an immediate and resounding "No!" As painful as it was to admit, she could no longer deny what had been true from the very beginning—Lauren now knew that she could no longer continue to see him and honor herself at the same time.

She finally realized that she'd never been a very high priority to this man; in fact, he'd been using her. In permitting this, she'd sent herself two very clearly destructive messages: "I don't deserve to be a priority," and "I don't value myself enough to insist on being treated well." But she was too "in love" to see what this was doing to her.

These messages were eating away at Lauren's happiness. It wasn't that she needed material things—what she really needed was acknowledgment and appreciation. She was feeling worse about herself and more at a loss about what to do to fix it. Ultimately, her unhappiness became too overwhelming to ignore.

In this way, Lauren had slowly but surely given away her dignity. She'd made all sorts of adjustments in *her* expectations in order to satisfy *his*. The result was that she'd profoundly dishonored herself, to the point of compromising her sense of her own worth and her ability to prioritize herself—a deadly combination in pursuing a relationship!

In spite of all that, she'd grown emotionally attached to this man. It was difficult for her, but she realized she had to leave in order to show herself—and the Universe—that she was truly valuable and deserved better. She ended the relationship, determined never to sacrifice her honor and dignity again.

The Choice Is Yours

The question I had asked Lauren was, "Does this relationship honor you?" This must be the question you ask yourself, not only concerning relationships, but concerning *everything* in your life. Ask yourself, "Does this honor me?" In other words, does this choice or situation bring honor to me and to my perception of myself? Does it make me *feel* honorable? Does it promote my sense of worth, value, and dignity, or does the choice I'm making diminish these feelings?

Since self-honoring is one of the most fundamental keys to your personal energy, it must become a major consideration in your life. If you begin to apply this question to every thought, choice, and action, you'll begin to make some very powerful—and very empowering—discoveries. If your behavior resonates with dishonoring choices, you won't be able to magnetize the happiness you desire. As with everything else, your choices determine the very direction of your destiny. Dishonoring choices magnetize dishonoring people and treatment—guaranteed.

> *How can you determine whether or not you are making choices that honor you? All your self-honoring choices will tend to promote your sense of dignity, personal and authentic power, and sense of balance. Sometimes the most self-honoring choices don't come easy and don't feel good at all. They may feel risky, difficult, and uncertain. Other times, the most self-honoring choices will feel completely natural to you—they'll feel exhilarating, giving you a sense of liberation and joyous self-actualization.*

See the Signs

Self-honoring choices create a balance between just feeling good and feeling good *about yourself*. You may have a very altruistic personality, tending to take care of others and putting their needs ahead of yours. Intellectually, you may feel good about yourself for all of that humanitarian energy. On a deeper level, however, you may be giving yourself the message, "I'm not worth putting myself and my life first. My needs aren't important. I'm not valuable enough to take care of myself."

Consistent repetition of these messages results in a profoundly negative effect on your personal energy field. People may appreciate your kindness, but it must be given in balance with compassion for yourself, or it will send the message, "I don't honor myself—you may dishonor me also."

The opposite type of focus is equally dishonoring. To be self-absorbed, arrogant, or easily enraged may make you feel good temporarily, but these things rarely feed your sense of dignity. In the long run, the message you're giving yourself (and others) is, "I'm not powerful just as I am. I have to find my power in anger, control, or pretending to be superior." Arrogance and hostility are essentially activities of compensation, designed to hide a deep emptiness that the person may not even be aware of. Such abrasive and unapproachable people actually sabotage their mistaken attempts at power, and attract revulsion and disgust instead.

Being passive and submissive is equally as dishonoring as being hostile and arrogant. If you find yourself in one of these categories, consider your intention. Are you motivated by fear, need, or obligation? If so, you'll never attract the kind of response you're looking for—which is a genuine appreciation for who you really are.

You must consistently choose to honor yourself throughout your daily life if you wish to create a healthy and attractive personal energy field. Even decisions or behaviors that have nothing to do with others can vibrate with very clear information about the way you honor yourself. What you prioritize, whether you engage in addictive behavior, how and with whom you choose to spend your time—all of these are ways you could honor or dishonor yourself without even realizing it.

Think about your habits. Do you overindulge in anything? Do you use people—in any way—to try to feel better about yourself? Do you use substances or activities to numb your pain or escape your boredom? How do you spend your time? Spending all your leisure time running around, performing endless tasks without any relaxation or pursuit of personal interests dishonors you just as much as spending all your time off sprawled on the couch watching television. *Real self-honoring requires a balance of responsibility, preference, and personal purpose.*

Real self-honoring choices include:

- *always* taking responsibility for yourself and your choices;

- being honest with yourself and others, even when it feels risky;

- allowing yourself to express emotions (including anger) *appropriately;*

- permitting yourself to have reasonable expectations within any relationship and being willing to express them;

- making decisions that show a reverence for your life, body, and physical and emotional health;

- being true to your spiritual values;

- having a healthy respect for your time, energy, and peace of mind;

- learning to accept *yourself and others* without judgment;

- desiring to be of service to others purely for the joy it brings to your life; and

- learning to be flexible and comfortable with change.

Ultimately, a self-honoring choice displays the highest regard for your dignity and your physical and emotional well-being. It also shows a strong determination *never* to sacrifice these things for the sake of a lesser, but perhaps more immediately gratifying, goal—such as creating or holding on to a relationship.

The Hidden Message

Another way to determine whether a choice honors or dishonors you is to ask yourself the question: "What's the message this choice is telling me about myself?" For example, what message are you sending yourself if you choose to pursue a relationship with a married person? Such a choice will invariably compromise your honor in some way. You may find ways to justify it, but the toxic messages that you send yourself, your partner, and the Universe are unavoidable and clearly demeaning. Such toxic messages include:

- "I don't deserve to be a priority in someone's life."

- "I'm not valuable enough, so I have to settle for being second best."

- "I have to follow someone else's agenda in order to have any relationship at all."

- "I'm not capable of attracting someone who would be willing to be there for me 100 percent. I have to settle for bits and pieces of time, attention, and emotional support."

- "I don't deserve to be loved completely."

What do you think these messages do to your self-love and personal energy? What do you think they're telling your partner about how much you respect and value yourself? Remember that you broadcast information about yourself in every choice, and that information determines who or what you'll attract. So even if you never verbalize these messages out loud, their energy will eventually poison everything about the relationship, even what you perceive to be good about it.

Without honor, virtually everything else in your life is empty, tainted, and superficial. Your choice to dishonor yourself eats away at your connection to your soul, and only unhappiness can move outward from that choice.

Another sensitive, yet significant, issue in the question of honoring choices concerns casual or unprotected sex. Intellectually, people know the risks, yet they tend to make all sorts of excuses. But a willingness to have unprotected sex in a new relationship virtually screams, "I don't value myself, my health, or my future." The message you're giving yourself and your lover—in spite of their reassurance or protestations—is that *their comfort and convenience are more important to you than your health and even your life*. Having "casual" sex devalues you, for sex is never casual—it's your most intimate and precious gift. One-night stands send the message that you don't value your own sexuality and you are not worth being taken seriously. Is that what you really want to say about yourself?

There are also many potentially **dishonoring choices** that may have nothing to do with romantic relationships, but you need to be aware of them if you really want to magnetize love, honor, and value into your life. Do you engage in any of the following? If so, what message do you think you're sending out?

Dishonoring choices include:

- lying, manipulating, or deceiving *in any way* to promote your own agenda, whether within a relationship or not;

- repeated judgment, humiliation, or criticism of self or others;

- belittling sarcasm, rage, or violence;

- excessive or inappropriate anger;

- using or abusing others or *allowing yourself* to be used or abused;

- refusing to take responsibility for yourself;

- blaming others or perceiving yourself as a victim;

- ignoring the needs of your body, mind, psyche, and spirit;

- rigidity or inflexibility; and

- overindulgence or addiction

Although some of these behaviors are *clearly* dishonoring, there are many situations where the self-honoring choice isn't so easy to distinguish. In fact, no one can actually determine for you what is self-honoring or not. The decision about what honors you can be found deep within you, in your intention, and in your intuition. You must listen to your heart, and you must be brutally honest with yourself when asking whether something you're engaging in is *really* honoring to you—and whether your intention behind it is honoring, too.

> *Honor and honesty have the same root word, and the two conditions can't be separated. If you refuse to take responsibility for your choices, you're lying to yourself about your own power. Real honesty requires courage and the ability to take risks. To have the magnetic energy that attracts really loving treatment, you must always have the courage to risk making the honest and self-honoring choice.*

Your refusal to honor yourself is based in need and fear. A devalued perception of yourself prompts you to manipulate, deceive, or overcompensate. Although the strategy may seem to work for a while, it only ends up perpetuating the very emptiness that your dishonoring choice is trying to fill.

Yet it's amazing how often we engage in dishonoring choices without even realizing it. We may be passive, take the easy way out, or play it safe. We may be manipulative, trying to promote our agenda in a fraudulent way. Or we may be forceful, domineering, and mean-spirited. In all of these approaches, we're unknowingly chipping away at our own self-esteem, making choices based on the underlying belief that we have no other option. Unfortunately, every time we act on that kind of assumption, we only magnetize more proof of it.

In such dishonoring choices, we are constantly sending ourselves toxic messages, such as:

- "I'm not worthy enough to speak out on my own behalf."

- "I must always make other people happy in order to be loved."

- "I need to be deceitful or manipulative to get what I want."

- "I have to overpower others or I'll have no power at all."

These kinds of messages create a dark consciousness in our personal energy. To the extent that we continue to engage in dishonoring choices, we carry that dark energy with us, either in subtle currents or in powerful blasts. Ultimately, it's that dark energy that colors the kind of treatment we'll attract from others. We're the source of our own hell or happiness *ourselves!*

Making *only* self-honoring choices brightens our consciousness and translates into strong, healthy messages to and about ourselves. Our energy of self-love flows freely outward, creating a current of love that will flow freely back.

Change Your Energy Now

To determine how honoring your choices are, think about any current situation or behavior you're involved in and ask, "Does this really honor me?" Apply this to all sorts of decisions, great and small, until it becomes a habit. *Don't take this lightly! This is the most dramatic thing you can do to improve your life.* The following steps will help in your process of self-honoring.

1. Take a moment to sense how you *feel* about your choice. Look for the emotional "red flags" that could indicate dishonoring—such as feelings of hurt, anger, or resentment; feeling used or minimized; or feeling a loss of dignity.

2. If your spontaneous emotion is one of these feelings, it's very likely that you're engaging in some sort of dishonoring choice or experience. Ask yourself what other options you may have in this situation that would be more self-honoring. *List all of them.* Entertaining these options may cause you to feel guilt, a sense of risk, or even a little fear. Often the most honoring thing we can do breaks our old patterns and leads us into unknown territory. *It takes courage.*

3. When you've listed your options, *pick the path that honors you,* even if it feels risky. You may wonder, "What if I get rejected?" or "What if someone gets mad?" Remind yourself that you *must* take the honoring path—the quality of your life will depend upon it.

4. Whenever possible, try to write about the situation and the many ways you could experience it. Ventilate your feelings. Practice how you would respond to the people involved. Make your *expressions* as self-honoring as your *choices.*

5. Meditate; ask for guidance. Ask your higher self to give you the courage to carry out your self-honoring response.

6. If people try to make you feel guilty or manipulate you in any way, remind yourself that *a truly self-honoring choice is never dishonoring to others.* It is *never* dishonoring to be truthful about your needs and feelings, when that truthfulness is expressed compassionately.

It's never dishonoring to be responsible for your own healthy attitude about yourself. If you can honestly answer in your heart of hearts, "Yes, this choice truly does honor me," then even if another may feel upset by your choice, in the long run it can only honor them, also.

Self-honoring isn't a form of selfishness or arrogance—it's important to make this distinction. Every being is a child of God, and to dishonor yourself is to deny that about you—to be arrogant is to deny that about others. It's time to bring this understanding into your life in very real ways. When you do, you'll feel the appreciation of the Universe in every honoring choice.

The Honoring Path

Here are some attitudes and affirmations that will help make self-honoring choices more of a way of life. Write some of your own. Repeat them often. Live their reality.

- *I deserve to make choices that honor me and maintain my self-respect.*

- *I always consider the energetic results of my choices and take responsibility for them.*

- *I deserve to be treated with respect and consideration within my relationships. I'm willing to voice this expectation whenever the need arises.*

- *As I make the choice to treat myself better, others will treat me better, also.*

- *I'm willing to speak out in my own behalf; I deserve my own support.*

- *From now on, I'll always consider what honors me—in my thoughts, words, and actions—and make that a priority.*

- *I express myself with confidence; I make choices of courage.*

- *Every day, in many situations, I ask myself, "Does this honor me?"*

- *I listen to my intuition and let it be my guide.*

- *I am learning to make decisions that show more respect for my body energy, and health.*

- *I stand up for myself. I assert my needs.*

- *I create balance and harmony by making balanced and harmonious choices.*

- *I am willing to take more risks in order to create more happiness in my life.*

- *I am one with the Universe. To honor myself is to honor the Universe. I'm courageous and capable.*

❧❀❧

The Law of Magnetism is real, present, and penetrating. Through it, you determine the direction of your life. It responds most positively when your choices demonstrate both a high regard for your fundamental worth and a deep awareness of your spiritual connection.

Your worth is your truth. To dishonor yourself is to live a lie. You must affirm your worth in your perception of yourself and in your self-talk. And you must demonstrate it consistently in the ongoing decisions you make throughout your life.

You can't force others to love or respect you through manipulation or submission. The only way you can attract real respect is by creating an energy of authentic—not arrogant—self-respect that resonates in your thoughts, words, actions, and reactions. *The kind of partner you are to yourself is the kind of partner you will magnetize to your life.*

The Law of Magnetism is strict but impartial. The Universe hates it when you hate yourself, because it has no choice but to return that energy to you. When you love yourself and choose to see yourself as the priceless eternal being that you are, the Universe rejoices and returns that love to you in a myriad of wonderful and unexpected ways.

But in order to get real commitment from others, you must *live* your commitment to yourself. *You must cultivate that commitment every day, in everything that you do and choose.* Know that a life of self-reverence leads to a greater current of reverence in the world. A refusal to diminish yourself is a refusal to diminish the current of appreciation in the world, and the Universe appreciates that!

Love *always* seeks to express and expand. The energy of pure love truly does desire to come your way. But you must first let it know that it has a welcome home in your heart; in your thoughts; and in your choices, actions, and reactions.

PART II

❧✿❧

The Laws of Desire and Intent

"Intention lays the groundwork for the effortless, spontaneous, frictionless flow of pure potentiality seeking expression from the unmanifest to the manifest."
— Deepak Chopra

Our desires bring a sense of purpose and direction to our life. They stimulate the wonderful energies of hope and excitement in our personal energy field. It is the pursuit of our desires that helps us connect with both our passion and our purpose.

Our intentions are our motivations. Every choice we make—from what to have for dinner to what career to pursue—is motivated by an underlying intention that, whether we are conscious of it or not, is based in a belief, emotion, or need. This is one of the strongest influences on our power of manifestation.

Desire is the starting point of every dream come true; intention determines if that dream becomes a vision or a nightmare.

❧ CHAPTER EIGHT ❧

Intending to Love

"Hope is the thing with feathers
That perches in the soul
And sings the tune without the words
And never stops—at all."
— Emily Dickinson

D esire is the wellspring of energy. It has been the source of phenomenal discoveries, spectacular art, and spellbinding literature and music. However, in its adulterated state, desire has also been the source of violence, destruction, betrayal, and even war.

Every human being desires romance—it's an innate need. When we combine a pure desire for love with a healthy intention, we accelerate the force of the Universal Laws and increase our energy of attraction. The **Law of Pure Desire** says that as long as we keep our intention pure and authentically motivated, a valuable, joyful result is assured. If, however, we contaminate our intention with fear, greed, negativity, or the desire for acquisition, we're no longer experiencing pure desire, but instead have shifted our energies to neediness and desperation.

Yet desire is necessary in every goal. It's the catalyst that moves us forward to the fulfillment of our dreams. It's the source of inspiration, the fountain of creativity, the compelling motivation to change.

There are five qualities engaged in the Law of Pure Desire—*hope, excitement, belief, deserving,* and *surrender.* While you might assume that all of these elements are natural and spontaneous responses to the feeling of desire, it's entirely possible that you may be lacking one or more of these qualities in the pursuit of your dreams. So it's important to understand the energies of each.

Hope and Excitement

Naturally, if you truly desire something, you'll be very hopeful about making it happen. *Hope* comes from knowing the benefits of your specific goal. Remind yourself often of those benefits; it will rekindle your hope and refocus your desire. You can even use visualization to repeatedly renew that initial hope. Picture yourself enjoying those benefits. Move your hope into an attitude of expectation. Affirm the possibilities.

Without hope, you will feel totally unmotivated. Your hopelessness will seep into your energy, creating lethargy and doubt. This stops you from moving into the next element, *excitement*—which infuses your desire with emotion. The more emotionally charged something is (whether good or bad), the more power it has in your life. When you're excited about a goal, you can *feel* it as a reality. It creates a joyous energy every time you think of it. This is an essential practice. *Excited visualization results in manifestation.*

Experiments in quantum physics are often done by *exciting* particles into action. The emotional charge that your excitement brings to your desire is vital for the same reason. It creates the energetic momentum, the action behind the desire. It pushes your intention forward with currents of vibration.

However, the excitement—and the resulting momentum—can be blocked if you have *conflicting intentions.*

You may actually feel hopeful about a certain goal, but instead of the resulting excitement, you may experience other feelings—such as dread, worry, or even anxiety. These feelings usually come from anticipating some other activity connected to the goal. For example, you may want to lose weight, but you may also dread the exercise and sense of deprivation that you expect to experience before accomplishing your desired results. You may wish to become a lawyer, but you may doubt your ability and experience uneasiness about the training required for that pursuit.

In the desire for romance, the concerns and worries that often temper the excitement are equally anxiety-provoking. They're based in such potentially catastrophic questions as: *What if I'm not good enough or attractive enough? What if I do or say the wrong thing, or trust the wrong person? What if I end up getting hurt again? What if I fail?* Such questions are guaranteed to sabotage not only your excitement, but your hopefulness—and ultimately the outcome of the desire itself.

> *To magnetize real love, you must make sure that your desire isn't driven by two conflicting intentions. You may desire romance, but may also wish to stay out of situations that could potentially hurt you. You may desire a healthy relationship but be unwilling to make the energetic changes that would bring one into your life. This creates a conflict in your intentions. Conflicted intentions can only result in a conflicted outcome!*

A client of mine was looking for a meaningful relationship, but he was extremely fearful of rejection. As a result, he continually chose women who were sure to accept him because they were so needy. He rarely based his choice on a genuine attraction, thinking that if the woman was too pretty, too smart, or in some way "superior" to him, he would never be able to hold on to her.

Inevitably he would find that he would lose interest. Since there was no chemistry with the women he did choose, he would have to break it off. He was always conflicted in this way. He never pursued the relationship he really wanted— and never really wanted the relationship he pursued.

This kind of confusion fragments both your *energy* and *intention*, the two most important factors that direct the powers of the Universal Laws. With conflicting intentions in your energy field, the Universe has no idea which intention to serve! You can, and *must,* prevent this confusion by fine-tuning your beliefs.

Belief and Deserving

In order to make your true desire a reality, you must engage in absolute *belief.* First and foremost, you must *believe* that you're capable of manifesting your goal. In a romantic goal, this means a full conviction in your capacity to love and be loved.

> *Your belief in your own value must be so strong that it translates into these conclusions: "I'm capable of loving and being loved. I deserve to be loved just as I am."*

If you don't feel these statements are true for you, you *must* continue to work on your perception of yourself, using the thought sheets, affirmations, and meditations described earlier. You *are* capable of making true love a reality. And no matter what you may have been taught to believe about yourself before, you absolutely deserve to be loved.

To deny that you're deserving of being loved dismisses your most special and spiritual legacy. It robs you of one of the primary purposes of life itself—to express and experience love. You must use every opportunity to create a strong sense of your belief in yourself and in your worthiness. Without this, your power of attraction will be greatly diminished.

Surrender

Surrender is the final quality of the Law of Pure Desire. This is often the missing piece in the puzzle, yet it's the amazing energizer that finally and totally opens up the Universe's abundant field of all possibilities.

> *As excited, hopeful, believing, and deserving as you may be, you must surrender your attachment to the outcome in order to make your greatest dreams come true. You must release your urgency and your need for control. Then your attitude of trust will actually accelerate the Universal Laws, helping the process along.*

Surrendering attachment to outcome doesn't mean giving up the desire. It means having enough trust in yourself and the Universe to know that *as you evolve, your energy will change, and you will rise to meet your greatest destiny.* In surrendering the outcome, you give it to a far more powerful director, one with limitless resources and creativity—the Universe itself! It's actually your *intention to surrender* that allows the Universe to orchestrate the optimum outcome for you.

Engaging in surrender is really quite liberating, because it means that you no longer have to control every variable in order to *make* your goal happen. This allows you to walk the fine line of intention between peaceful acceptance and active pursuit, to decide without desperation, to focus without fear. Whatever your goal is, surrendering the *need* to make it happen speeds up the current of manifestation. With surrender, you take the action and release it with trust—to the *open outcome* of your desire. This is the spiritual path of peaceful pursuit.

Without this surrender, you'll constantly be striving, fighting the tide, meeting resistance upon resistance, and always wondering why it has to be so difficult. What isn't clear, however, is that the difficulty is actually generated by your lack of trust—and your refusal to let go.

Purpose and Paradox

Whether or not you're able to surrender to the open outcome of your desire will depend upon the *purpose* you *intend* the outcome to serve for you. You may desire a relationship because you want to expand the experience of love in your life and you want to share your joy and dreams with another. In these cases, your purpose aligns itself with the Universal intention of love.

But be careful; your purpose in pursuing a romance may have other underlying unhealthy intentions, such as defining who you are, increasing your worth, or making you feel better about yourself. It may be intended to win the approval of others or to ensure personal or financial security. *These intentions are fear-based and they contaminate your desire.* Since they don't align with the Universe's intention to spread love, you'll find it very difficult to create the happy, long-lasting relationship you're looking for.

Real love—and every other good thing—can be poisoned by fear. This is why it's important to look very closely at the *energy and intentions* behind every desire. If your motivation is based in fear, it can move you out of the beneficial effects of the Law of Pure Desire and into the difficult realm of the **Law of Paradoxical Intent.**

*The Law of Paradoxical Intent says the more des-
perate your intention to achieve a certain goal, the
more you sabotage your efforts and push your desired
outcome away. Conversely, the Law of Pure Desire says
the greater your intent to trust and surrender, the more
you'll draw that desire to you. The Laws of Pure Desire
and Paradoxical Intent, like all Universal Laws, follow
consistent patterns in response to the driving forces of
your needs and motivations.*

Taking the Tension out of Intention

Life decisions may appear similar on the surface, but deeper investigation often reveals very different qualities of energy and intent. This creates vastly different results according to the dynamics of the Universal Laws. For example, a person who makes the decision to marry based only on love, with an intention to honor self and partner, will magnetize a wonderful marriage experience, full of joy and excitement. Yet a person who decides to marry out of need, emptiness, or fear of being alone engages in an intention to control or acquire. This person, although making the same decision, will magnetize a vastly different marriage experience, one that's likely to be lonely or filled with conflict. *Intentions based in fear will always result in constriction, longing, or lack of some kind.*

To release ourselves from the problems of paradoxical intent, we must replace our urgency with trust. By engaging in striving and urgency, we actually magnetize the paradox of our intent, *reversing* our hoped-for outcomes! The more desperate our desires, the more unhappy our energy, and therefore the more unhappy the results.

The key element here is *desperation. Desperation occurs when desire is coupled with fear or urgency.* The need to be *certain* of our intended outcome creates a compulsion to worry and hurry through our process. This is a surefire way to ensure all sorts of problems with the result—if not to prevent the outcome all together.

I know a woman who is desperate to be married. She's actually been engaged several times, and each time it has fallen through. Every time she gets close to a man, she gets clingy and demanding, so much so that the man can't help but want to get away. She projects an energy of fear—so the man becomes afraid of her! The paradox is, if she doesn't change her desperate *need* to marry, she'll never be able to make her *intention* to marry a reality.

This is the demand of the Law of Paradoxical Intent. You must replace desperation with a peaceful mind and an attitude of trust. Without this trusting attitude, your urgency will only push your desired outcome away. Even if you should ultimately achieve the desired outcome, you'll find that it will never provide the positive emotional experience that you were hoping for.

With Love from the Universe

Why should this happen? Why would the Universe not want us to achieve the very thing we so desperately want? Actually, the Universe *longs* to fulfill our fondest dreams—it's not the law that's the problem, it's our own attitude. In reality, the Law of Paradoxical Intent is designed to protect us from creating our own unhappiness—in two very important ways.

Its first form of protection comes in causing us to release our desperation. It forces us to think about the underlying assumption behind our neediness. Desperation takes away our power and implies that we're not able to make ourselves happy, which causes us to give up our responsibility to do so.

In being *desperate,* we make basic assumptions that are dishonoring to us, such as, "Without a relationship, I can never be happy (or feel valuable, worthy, or safe)." This subconsciously tells us, *"Until I make this a reality, everything else is meaningless."*

With such an overwhelming sense of lack, it's truly *impossible* to be happy in our current circumstances, in the present moment! Our desperation becomes our perception of reality, and our dishonoring conclusion easily becomes a self-fulfilling prophecy.

In its infinite wisdom, the Universe won't let you do this to yourself. It has no intention of helping you throw away your present, or letting you connect your value to any external condition. *It simply won't allow you to abandon a life of happiness now while waiting for some unknown "condition of happiness" to appear in the future.*

The law of gravity is designed to keep you grounded in your physical reality. Similarly, the Laws of Desire and Intent help keep you grounded in your spiritual and essential truth. You are—by essence—a manifestation of God's Love on Earth, a vessel of potential happiness by nature of this gift. The opportunity for a joyous life is *always* available to you through this Divine connection. Obsessing about *any* earthly desire turns you away from the present joy that brilliant connection can bring. And being desperate causes you to see only what you're missing, which makes you feel empty and alone. When this happens, the Universal Laws say, "No way!" The Universe wants you to *be happy now*, not just hope for happiness later.

Desperation eradicates the potential for joy in your daily life. You feel miserable because you're "deprived" of something you're convinced is necessary for your happiness. With desperation, your personal energy field resonates with urgency and need, making it impossible to magnetize the happy relationship—or anything else—that you're aching to achieve. Instead of peaceful self-respect being your predominant frequency, what you're actually sending out is wave after wave of fear. The resulting consequence of this is to attract either someone who is equally fearful or someone who will delight in feeding off your fear for their own sense of power. In either event, the energy of desperation that makes you miserable while waiting for the relationship will make you equally miserable once you get it.

The Law of Paradoxical Intent is unwilling to allow you to live in the agony of desperation, relegating your happiness to some future conditional event. It teaches you how powerful you really are when you discover that your thoughts have the ability to draw or to block your own coveted outcomes. It protects you by *forcing* you to release the fear that both contaminates your present and prevents you from attracting the dreams of your future. In its insistence that you engage in an attitude of happiness *now*, it changes your energy. This stimulates the Universal powers and causes you to attract even more happiness in the future.

Opening the Golden Door

The second way the Law of Paradoxical Intent protects you is by opening up your willingness to see other options. Desperation is a very limiting energy. It causes you to focus all of your thoughts, energy, and emotions on one very specific goal, believing that it's the *only* way to be happy. This creates an obsession that closes your mind to other options for real happiness. Like a horse with blinders on, your focus is straight ahead toward one desired outcome only. You're blind to other possible roads to happiness—especially the potential for experiencing happiness as a matter of choice rather than condition.

Letting go of this narrow-minded obsession, however, exposes you to the opportunity for joy in any given moment. And it reveals the potential for happiness in *many more* experiences than your limited, obsessive focus could ever reveal.

I'm sure you can recall someone who was absolutely convinced that they had to have a certain person in their life in order to be happy. Yet circumstances (or more likely their own desperate energy) prevented that from happening. Later, when the situation played itself out, they realized that they were actually happier because they did *not* get the results they had originally wanted! Perhaps this has even happened to you—when you finally let go and moved on, you were able to see how protected you were when you didn't get what you were so determined to have.

Whatever you may be obsessing about now, try to remember that you're narrowing your options. The Universe is a wealth of abundance and joy, and there are truly limitless numbers of potential outcomes that can bring you phenomenal happiness, many of which you may have never even considered before.

Living with desperation and limitation is like living in the dark. You stumble around, reaching out joylessly for all that eludes you. Meanwhile, you keep banging into the blessings of your present life, cursing them because you're blind to their real value. But when you release desperation, you enlighten yourself to all the wonders that your life has to offer. You're in the *great field of all possibilities*—the Universe's brilliant and plentiful storehouse of unlimited resources—and there are many wonderful options to look into and enjoy!

If, as the Law of Paradoxical Intent directs, you can be *open* to pursuing these options and be *patient* for the outcome, then you can rest assured that *your desires are already being met in the energetic world.* Trust and let go. It's only a matter of time before your new energy brings your desires to you—and your greatest dreams really do come true!

Change Your Energy Now

If you want to ignite the energies of the Law of Pure Desire, remember the five key elements. Don't limit your implementation of them to a mere intellectual under-standing. Instead, create a real feeling for each of them. Make them a part of your life, a part of how you approach each day.

1. Maintain your *hopes*. Never let go of your dreams—smile when you think of them. Send your hopeful energy out into the Universe, and see it sparkle with possibility.

2. Let yourself get *excited!* Visualize the end results and *feel* the excitement of their reality welling up in you. Do this often; it's a powerful way to energize your goals.

3. Affirm your *belief* in yourself and in the achievement of your goal. Put your affirma-tions in the present tense: *I'm a valuable part-ner. I'm attracting love. I have a great relationship!*

4. Affirm that you are *deserving!* Know that you're worthy of truly great things. Remember, you receive what you believe.

5. *Surrender* any attachment or investment in the outcome. Be patient and live with trust. If you try to force the harvest, you end up killing the crop.

In order to avoid the energy of Paradoxical Intent, you must review your reasons for pursuing your desire. Your intention is such a powerful force in the achievement of your desire, it can't be overstated. *Just by creating the intention, you start the Universal energies moving.* Affirm it. Write it. Envision it! All of this will accelerate the process—that is, of course, if the intention is based in love, not fear.

What are your real intentions? Are they loving and honoring, or are they needy and desperate? If they're the latter, you're bound to push your desire away. Approach your desires with these three directives:

1. *Take responsibility for your own happiness,* now and always.

2. *Open yourself up to the many opportunities for joy* that your life already has to offer.

3. *Let go of desperation!* Don't obsess about only one desired outcome. Let the Universe send its unlimited treasures your way!

❧ CHAPTER NINE ❧

Codependency and Paradoxical Intent

The Codependent Blues

"He's the worst damn man that ever came my way.
I would leave him, if I loved him,
but I hate him, so I'll stay."
— Anonymous

Maggie consulted me a year after beginning a new relationship. Her previous relationship had ended in a very painful breakup, and she still carried the fear of that experience with her. That fear turned into despondency, moving her from purity of desire to desperate intent, threatening her new love.

The beginning of the relationship had been blissful. She and her boyfriend, Jack, had gotten very close, very quickly. They truly enjoyed each other's company, but soon he told her that things were moving too fast. She became so scared of losing him that she started to become obsessed. No one would have believed this about Maggie. She was a very popular television personality. Her public appearances elicited the adulation of countless men, but that didn't seem to matter. Once she started dating a man, she embarked on a mission to make him love her—with the ultimate goal of marriage.

Maggie's Story

When she was growing up, Maggie's family had consistently given her the message that a woman's only real happiness came from being married and having a family. In spite of the fact that Maggie was happy with her life, her relatives continued to imply that something was missing. They kept asking her, "When are you going to get married?"

Both of her sisters were married with children, and this fact was constantly thrown up at her in any number of subtle—and not so subtle—ways. The expectation had eaten away at her for years and was the basis for all of the fear patterns she'd developed concerning relationships. For instance, Maggie constantly doubted her value as a partner. It happened that Jack was a very handsome man, and this frightened her. In spite of her own good looks, she thought she would never be good enough to keep him.

Maggie began scrutinizing Jack's activities, feeling that she had to keep tabs on whomever he was spending his time with. Although he never knew it, she often made it a point to drive by his house to see if he was home. She gauged the condition of the relationship by his moods and behaviors, always drawing the *negative and catastrophic* conclusion—if Jack was tired and wanted to spend an evening alone, she'd interpret this to mean he wanted to break up. If he spoke to a good-looking woman, it meant that Maggie wasn't attractive enough for him.

Needless to say, by the end of the first year, Jack was pulling away from Maggie. Although she hadn't directly revealed her fears to him, his reaction was an inevitable response to her own personal energy. In spite of the fact that he'd come to care for her very deeply, he'd begun expressing the need for more time alone, and more "space."

Early on, Maggie had decided that she would play it any way Jack wanted—she thought it was the only way to keep him. So if she got to see him less and less often now, she'd be willing to do so. She rarely requested anything of him, setting up a dangerous precedent in terms of how she was willing to be treated.

Maggie's Plan

Maggie was miserable, and she knew she'd have to make some major changes. First, she *had to* change the countless desperate and destructive conclusions she'd made about herself—and about relationships in general. For instance, her thoughts demonstrated incredible neediness. She believed that she needed Jack to be happy, and that she alone was responsible for making the relationship work. She believed that his needs were more important than hers, so she had to put him first.

We attacked these and other beliefs by using the thought-restructuring approach described in Chapter 2. She listed all of her toxic conclusions and then replaced them with new ones that affirmed her value and power. Some of her new beliefs included:

- *I create my own happiness. I take responsibility for my happiness every day.*

- *My value is intrinsic to myself and doesn't depend on Jack.*

- *Jack is responsible for his own happiness, and I am responsible for mine.*

- *I don't need to fix his emotions. We each take responsibility for our own feelings.*

Maggie needed to accept herself and let go of her need to control everything. These were strong patterns and weren't going to change overnight. She continued to do thought sheets as well as affirmations, inundating herself with this new, healthy thinking and optimistic energy.

Maggie's next goal called for new behaviors. We made a list of the things that she'd have to do differently from that point on. They included:

1. Not calling Jack as often; letting go of the need to get his input in order to feel safe or happy.

2. Expressing her feelings and letting him take some of the responsibility for the direction of the relationship.

3. Not driving by his house—no matter what! (She always felt a great loss of dignity when engaging in this behavior.)

4. Spending time alone, getting involved in other interesting activities.

5. Telling her family that she needed to be acknowledged and accepted for herself; requesting that they no longer ask her when she would be getting married.

Maggie took these adjustments very seriously, although the changes were difficult at first. She saw how desperate she'd become, and she made a vow to change everything that promoted that despairing energy once and for all.

The final change she would have to make, however, was the most difficult. Maggie now knew that she'd have to be willing to surrender her extreme attachment to the relationship, even if that meant surrendering the relationship itself—it could no longer be more important than her self-respect, dignity, or happiness. After all, the reason she sought the relationship in the first place was because she thought it would bring her happiness. In truth, she'd made herself miserable over it!

During this time, Jack was out of town quite a bit and less available than ever. Even when they were together, he wasn't very attentive or affectionate. Maggie had finally developed truly reasonable expectations—and even they weren't being met. Jack had become distant and the relationship empty; so Maggie felt that her only self-honoring option was to get out.

As much as it pained her to do so, Maggie told Jack that they would have to break up. She expressed herself calmly and maintained her dignity. She told him that she not only needed more from him, but she also needed more from herself. They stopped dating, and her grief was overwhelming. She was constantly tempted to call him, but instead, she wrote about it in her journal, getting her feelings out and trying to fortify her new understanding. *She* would be the source of her happiness from now on.

In time, Maggie began feeling a strength and peacefulness that she hadn't felt in a long time. Her choice to trust and value herself gave her the serenity that she'd always been hoping her relationships would provide. She hadn't realized it, but Maggie's approach to relationships had displayed a strong tendency towards being codependent.

At first, the term *codependency* referred to a person who was dependent on someone with an addiction. Over time, though, it's come to mean anyone who has a dependency on either one specific relationship or on relationships in general. Codependency is an addiction itself—an addiction to relationships. And like all addictions, the substance eventually becomes toxic to the user.

Codependent people often attach their very identity to the existence of their relationship. They feel a desperate need to be within a relationship when they're alone, and when they *are* in a relationship, a constant sense of insecurity plagues them with the need to maintain it. These problems of codependency are very closely connected with the problems of paradoxical intent. Learning to release codependency, therefore, is necessary in shifting your energies from the desperation of paradoxical intent to the sweet surrender of pure desire. To do that, you must first recognize the signs.

The Emotional Signs of Codependency

There are many common emotional clues that signal one's tendency to be codependent. The first signals are *fear* and a *need for certainty*. The basic fears are "What if this doesn't work?" "What if I get rejected?" or "What if I never have a committed relationship?"

If you feel fear about your relationship, you'll always be looking for evidence in your partner's words and behaviors to reassure you. This creates incredible urgency, the constant need to be certain *now* about the future. The codependent person falsely believes that absolute certainty about the future is possible and can come from controlling the present.

This *need for control* is another emotional sign. The truly codependent person wants to control most of the variables in the other person's life. The primary goal is establishing and maintaining the relationship at all costs, which requires ceaseless monitoring of such things as the partner's plans, social activities, even phone calls. This reaction often extends to needing to control the partner's feelings. In extreme cases, a codependent person may not even want the partner to be happy unless they're together. The need for all the partner's attention and affection can often give rise to feelings of jealousy and proprietorship.

This constant *worry* can create an overall sense of agitation that stimulates the other emotional signs of *brooding* and *obsessive analyzing* about the relationship. This becomes the major focus, creating a loss of balance and ultimately a *loss* of control.

The emotional signals of codependency are:

- a need for certainty;
- a need for control;
- fear and worry; and
- brooding and obsessive analysis.

These are all stimulators of the Law of Paradoxical Intent. The toxic energy of these emotions will sabotage the very desire that drives them. If you're experiencing any of these emotional signals in dealing with relationships, you're probably codependent. Your fearful energy not only eats away at your own happiness, it poisons the potential happiness the relationship could bring.

The Behavioral Signs of Codependency

There are also *behavioral signals* that indicate a tendency to be codependent. The first and most obvious one is the chronic *adjustment* of one's own priorities and preferences in order to please the other person. This may start out very subtly, but over time it can be an insidious disease to the self-esteem.

People often start relationships by changing little things about themselves in order to please their partners. It may be as simple as how they dress, what they eat, or the kind of people they hang around with—but it all adds up in time. Eventually the pattern of adjustment calls for them to ignore their own needs when they contradict their partner's in any way. Left unchecked, this leads to a devastating sense of loss and self-betrayal.

Another signal of codependency is an *imbalance* in the energy and attention given to the relationship. Many clients have said to me, "I have to initiate all of the activity, or else we'd never get together." If this truly is the case, then perhaps you shouldn't be getting together. Since no two people have the same nature or the same ways of expressing themselves, it would be unreasonable to expect the effort, energy, and interest in the relationship to be equally displayed 100 percent of the time. However, if there is a consistent lack of balance in effort and attention, the result will be feelings of resentment for one's partner and eventually for oneself.

Some common patterns of imbalance include: making most of the phone calls, planning most of the activities, and performing most of the mundane tasks that should be shared. In addition, a very deep resentment can develop from an imbalance of affection. This includes: being the one to do most of the caring things—including giving gifts, acknowledging the other, demonstrating appreciation, expressing love and affection, and even initiating sex.

This signal of imbalance is closely related to the signal of *sacrifice*. The one who tends to *do* the most in the relationship also tends to *sacrifice* the most. This can create a loss of identity and personal perspective. It occurs when there's a willingness to abandon personal pursuits—and it can extend to sacrificing your own family and social life in deference to what you perceive to be your partner's needs.

It's not uncommon for people to focus much of their energy on a new relationship—there's an excitement and enthusiasm that lifts people out of their personal routine. While this is a very normal reaction, it can actually be a dangerous precedent to set.

It's important—even at the beginning—to maintain a significant amount of personal time in which you continue to pursue your own interests and engage in your own social activities. Never lose sight of the special things that make you you. These are the things that caused your partner to fall in love with you. If you give them up, even at the request of your partner, you'll

*lose that unique energetic attraction that brought the
two of you together in the first place.*

The Energy of Attachment

Another behavioral signal of codependency is the *inability to disengage* when it's clear that there's no longer any reciprocity of feeling. The similarities between addiction and codependency become very apparent when one partner has indicated that the relationship is over and the other partner continues to engage in the pursuit. The relationship has become like an addictive substance that the person simply can't give up, no matter how futile the situation may be.

There are two very important energetic problems that take place when one person refuses to give up an attachment even after there's no longer any loving or reciprocal connection. First, it's the ultimate energy of dishonoring. The message you're sending in pursuing an unrequited relationship is tantamount to begging—it screams desperation and a willingness settle for a loveless connection.

Second, the inability to disengage ties up your energy and confuses your intention. You may be saying that you want a new relationship, but if you're pining after a lost (even long-lost) love, the Universe already sees a connection there and isn't compelled to respond. Even if you haven't seen the person for years, if you're still emotionally attached, the message you're sending to potentially new romantic energies is "Not available. Don't come here."

I've had several clients come to me long after the breakup of their relationship, saying, "I can't stop thinking about him" or "Nobody measures up to her. I have to have her back."

When I ask if the relationship is likely to be rekindled, their honest response is "No." Yet something keeps them hanging on—usually a lingering hope, overwhelming grief, or unexpressed anger.

If you find yourself in this type of situation, rest assured that until you finally release the unfinished emotions and clear these tangled-up attachments, your attempts at finding true love will be frustrating at best. You must create an intention to let it go. Express your grief or anger—even if it was a long time ago. When longing thoughts come up, breathe deeply and release them. Affirm that there are wonderful relationships in store for you. They'll come closer as you continue to put this behind you. Open yourself to new and better opportunities.

Finally, one of the most alarming and unhealthy behaviors that clearly indicate codependency is *manipulation*. Manipulation is the attempt to get what you want by fraudulent, sneaky, or underhanded means. This includes fabricating reasons to get together, lying about *anything*—including one's income, age, career, or marital status—and inventing ways to engender jealousy, fear, intimidation, or need in one's partner. Manipulative behaviors are a threat to your integrity, and anything that compromises your integrity dishonors you. Anything that smacks of scheming, "guilting," lying, or deceiving to promote your agenda is manipulative and will eventually sabotage your efforts. It puts into play the Universal forces that can *only* bring deceit and duplicity back to you.

When we look at these behaviors, it's very clear how unhealthy and destructive we can become in our pursuit of love. By engaging in these codependent behaviors, we willingly, although perhaps unknowingly, relinquish our own personal dignity. We subjugate it to the priority of the relationship, never realizing that without our dignity, every relationship is false. Without our dignity, any sense of security, appreciation, or priority within the relationship is untrue.

When we abandon our dignity, all we're left with
is a compelling sensation of emptiness and an over-
whelming sense of lack. As a result, we can never really

feel secure. Whatever we have within the relationship is an illusion. Since we know our relationship is built on a lie, we're destined to always feel scared and empty. No relationship, addiction, or acquisition will ever be powerful enough to fill a heart without dignity. In fact, there will never be enough of anything to fill the heart that has lost its honor.

Why do we set ourselves up for such misery? *We pursue a relationship because we intend to be happy.* In time, the pursuit becomes so important that we're willing to dismiss our honor to force it to happen. We end up feeling isolated, confused, and unappreciated. *In such a state, we cannot possibly be happy. We have created the paradox of our intent!*

Happy Ending

Let's get back to Maggie. She'd worked herself up into a frenzy over Jack, and her urgency had pushed him away. She grieved the loss of the relationship, but she let it go and decided to approach her life differently. She worked on redefining herself and establishing a strong autonomy. She did daily affirmations about having a bright future and being worthy of love. *She totally changed her focus from fear to value,* and she finally found real worth on her own.

About three months after their breakup, Maggie heard from Jack. As it often happens with the Law of Paradoxical Intent, when she genuinely let go of the desperation, that which she desired finally appeared. Jack told her that he missed her and wanted her back in his life. They talked openly about what had happened between them—Maggie told Jack that she needed him to be more available, and Jack confessed that he'd tried to create some distance due to a difficult divorce. Both began to understand more about themselves—and about each other.

When Maggie and Jack started dating again, she repeatedly reminded herself, *"I can do this relationship differently,"* which was a very helpful affirmation for her because it often gave her the strength, courage, and determination she needed to let go of her old codependent patterns.

Maggie maintained her autonomy, seeing her friends and engaging in her own individual pursuits. She *refused* to worry or obsess, and she always behaved with dignity. She made self-honoring choices, expressing her needs and taking action on her own behalf. In fact, Maggie realized that she'd *never before approached a relationship in this healthy way.* For the first time in her relationship experience, she felt hopeful, confident, and in control. She indeed could and would do this relationship differently.

She and Jack are building a life together now. All that she was so desperate to achieve before is happening now because she finally made the decision to honor herself and let the desperation go. The Universal Laws, as always, responded to the shift in her energy and intention. She let go of the attachment, and the outcome came through!

I have never seen this combination of self-love and surrendering fail. Make it your top priority to always honor yourself. Surrender the need and live in trust. This will dramatically change your energy—as well as everything you magnetize in return. This is the formula for finding and keeping real love. You must be willing to depend on yourself first. Your own heart is the genesis of love—in all the Universe, there's no other place to start!

❧ ❦ ❧

❧ Chapter Ten ❧

Life Under Construction

*"The happiness which we receive from ourselves
is greater than that which we obtain from our
surrounding . . . The world in which a man lives
shapes itself chiefly by the way in which he looks at it."*
— Arthur Schopenhauer

What is the source of our emotional chaos? What is the motivation that leads us to desperation? Whether we realize it or not, we're always driven by our psychological "constructs." We create a *construct* when we connect a state of mind to an external event. Our basic constructs revolve around our happiness, value, self-acceptance, or security—and to these emotional states we usually attach the achievement of very specific goals. We then become *driven* to attain those goals in order to ensure the desired state of being. Constructs always read according to the format, "If A, then B." The most common constructs that people engage in concern relationships and money. These include:

- "I need *to be married* to be *happy*."

- "A *relationship* will make me more *valuable* and *acceptable*."

- "Things will be *secure* when I have a *better job* or *more money*."

- "Life would be so much *better* if I had a *partner*."

You can see the toxic connections that can be drawn between states of mind and external achievements. Unfortunately, engaging in these constructs, even at a subconscious level, can only result in the formation of the corresponding but opposite negative constructs, such as:

- "I *can't be happy* unless I'm *married*."

- "I'm *not valuable* and people *won't accept me* if I am *alone*."

- "I'll *never be* truly *secure* until I have *more money*."

- "Life is *miserable without* a *partner*."

These driving assumptions, even if they're unconscious, actually destroy our desires. As a result, our happiness (or unhappiness) constructs can determine the very quality of our lives. When we *really believe* we'll never be happy without a relationship, the *belief* itself is so very disturbing that it *creates* the very misery we're trying to avoid!

Lack or Love?

The predominant energy behind this process of construction comes from an *attitude of lack*. We create the energy of lack in our lives, not from the reality of our circumstances, but from how we interpret our circumstances.

There are many people who constantly focus on the things they're lacking—yet to an outside observer, they would appear to have blessed lives. There are others who may not have very much, yet in spite of what may be missing from their lives, they rarely concern themselves with what they lack. Instead, they focus on what they have to enjoy. Such an approach is based on an *attitude of love* and the intent to value.

> *Lack and love are the two basic filters through which we interpret most of our life experiences. Lack is fear-based and projects a consciousness filled with need and longing. An attitude of lack dismisses the present value. Love, on the other hand, is the emotion of appreciation. An attitude of love not only sees the present value, but actively seeks it out in everyday life.*

If our lives are filled with constructs such as, "I need this to be happy, or that to be safe," we're interpreting our experiences as evidence of lack. However, when we already perceive our lives and ourselves as being full of value—when we're consciously aware of the peace, beauty, leisure, joy, or even adventure in life—we are appreciating our experiences. They are evidence of love, from the Universe, from each other, and from ourselves.

According to the Law of Magnetism, *that which you focus on expands*. With this in mind, the following questions should indicate your real focus.

1. Do you seek to obtain what you lack, or do you seek to enjoy—even *love*—what you have?

2. How much of your time do you spend worrying about what's wrong instead of focusing on what's right?

3. If you could change anything in your life, would you change the things that you worry about, or would you change the fact that you worry at all?

Look at your answers—is the energy of lack the pre-dominant focus in your life? Is this what you want to expand in your experiences?

Name Your Poison

There are several basic issues that tend to bring out con-cerns of lack in most people. The most common is *money*. It wouldn't, of course, be unnatural for most of us to want more money, but remember that a pure desire doesn't engage in urgency or striving. You can desire more money without feeling you're lacking in what you have. When you look at your financial situation with desperation—or when you look at another's wealth with envy or resentment—your focus is one of lack.

An extension of this particular issue is the acquisition of *material things*. While you may like to have a nicer home, a better car, or fancier clothes, when you use these things as a way to value yourself, again your focus turns to lack. You are always more than what you possess, even if you could possess the entire world!

Some people think they come up short in the *looks* department. They obsess about their weight, hair, or fea-tures—instead of seeing the beauty of their souls, they focus on the physical things they'd like to change about them-selves. Consequently, they always feel unhappy with their appearance.

Intellect is another area where people tend to focus on their deficiencies. They judge themselves for not being clever or even educated enough. They worry about what peo-ple think about their opinions, insights, work performances, or mental acumen. A *sense of humor* is a variation on this issue. Many people feel they lack a quick wit, and judge themselves for not being spontaneous or funny enough. But the Law of Paradoxical Intent is especially clear when it comes to *performance* of mind or body. *The more you worry about your performance, whether mental or physical, the more the resulting tension is sure to sabotage the outcome.*

Many people feel that they lack *confidence*. They worry about their social skills, often wondering if they've said the right thing, behaved in the right way, or acted appropriately in any given situation. Instead of just *being themselves,* they're always *second-guessing* themselves and worrying about what kind of impression they have left.

Take this friend of mine, for instance. She called me one night and said, "I figured out why I have so much trouble dating. I have no social skills." I was speechless—I'd known this woman for ten years and had seen her in every type of social situation. There was nothing she couldn't handle, yet when it came to dating, she felt no confidence. She'd been harboring this fear, allowing it to make her feel awkward, ill prepared, and tense whenever she went out.

Second to money, the thing that people feel they lack the most is *love.* They feel that the presence of love is either minimal or totally absent in their lives. They rarely see its potential in their friends and family, and what's worse, they *never* acknowledge its presence within themselves. They see their lives as empty and destined to be loveless forever. They rarely extend themselves because they're sure that it's useless—and again the energy of their assumption turns into a self-fulfilling prophecy.

The last and most important area where people tend to assume lack is in their *personal value.* This may not be as apparent as the nagging obsessions about their lack of money or love, but it's just as insidious, and far more critical. People often think there is a fundamental lack within their character, that something is missing, which makes them less deserving or less worthy, and diminishes them in relation to everybody else.

Some people can't pinpoint exactly why it is that they feel this way, while others can recite long lists of precisely what is wrong with them. Focusing on what you don't have in this area is likely to cause the assumption of lack regarding most of the other issues on the list. It's one of the most toxic things you can do to yourself and your magnetic energy. *Your personal value is an intrinsic part of who you are and cannot be diminished. This must be firmly established if you want to attract more value to your life.*

Whatever your personal issues are, if your habit is to perceive lack, what do you think you will magnetize in return? If your predominant focus is on what you don't have, then the only thing that can expand in your life is lack itself.

The Value in Valuing

Instead of devoting yourself to the *energy* of scarcity, you do have the option to focus on love—to appreciate instead of condemn. And you also have the option to interpret your experiences, whatever they may be, with some amount of acceptance and satisfaction.

To choose love is to embrace value. If you think of anything or anyone that you've loved, you'll realize that there was a strong recognition of value there. Whether it was a certain kind of music, a hot fudge sundae, or your favorite sweater, when you say, "I just love that," what you mean is, "I value this. This experience brings joy and appreciation to my life."

When you love a person—whether it's a spouse, parent, child, or friend—you experience the sensation of love because you have a heartfelt recognition of their value in your life. This is, in fact, where love begins—in the recognition and appreciation of value!

So you can see how important this issue is. The attitudes of lack and love are vastly different, and they create vastly different consequences in your life.

Love vs. Lack

- Love is the intention to appreciate. Lack is the intention to judge. When you release judgment, you perceive your life with peace. When you hold on to judgment, you perceive only problems.

- Love trusts in the natural evolution of things, and flows through the process of life with faith and flexibility. Lack always has an agenda, a striving, fighting approach to life; and it always feels the need to compete, to control, and attempt to acquire.

- Love sees the value in everything. Lack misses the value in pretty much anything.

- Love embraces life with acceptance. Lack dismisses, destroys, and denies.

- Love attracts. Lack repels.

- Love finds. Lack never stops seeking.

Which of these approaches would you take? Choose love and you'll focus on all that you already have to value—choose lack and you'll always be desperate about needing something. Your choice determines your very destiny. This is why it's so important to understand what your predominant focus is all about. How much valuing or lacking does your mind engage in each day? Spend some time keeping track. You may be surprised when you find out just how much energy you devote to the experience of lack.

Change Your Energy Now

There's a reason why so many of us perceive our lives to be *full of emptiness.* All it takes is a few basic constructs of lack to expand into an entire network of damaging assumptions. Try to identify your own. Which of the following toxic thoughts and relationship constructs do you engage in? Intervene on them *whenever* they come up.

- "I have to have this (or any) relationship to define myself. I'm nothing without it."

- "Someone else must provide me with the approval I need to be happy."

- "I'm not complete as I am; I'm missing something I need."

- "I need to do whatever my partner wants to keep getting their approval."

- "I need to always be on guard to notice changes in my partner's behavior and moods. I have to watch for signs that something is wrong."

- "It's always my responsibility to fix things when they go wrong and to make sure the relationship is going well."

- "People will think less of me if I'm alone."

- "I will think less of myself if I'm alone."

- "If I lose this relationship, it means there's something wrong with me."

- "If I lose this relationship, I'll never find another one like it."

- "If I haven't had a relationship in a while, there's *really* something wrong with me."

- "If I don't have a relationship now, I'll *never* be able to find one."

Every single one of these statements is an assumption of lack. They're so clearly *devaluing* that it's impossible to engender *any* joy or peace of mind based on their energy. As long as you maintain this line of thinking, you become caught in a bizarre process. You devalue yourself in the present, assuming your only value can come in the future. This negates your magnetic energy, making it *impossible* to attract that valuable future!

Moving into Love

You need to stop this vicious cycle of expanding negative energy. In order to change your relationship energy from the desperation of lack to the pure desire of love, you *must* start with your basic constructs. It doesn't matter how these old beliefs have come to you, or even how firmly you believe them to be true, you *must* be willing to change them if you want to manifest more value in your life. You *must* embrace the following new beliefs, and take the action to make them real.

- *I always create happiness in my life, whether I'm in a relationship or not.*

- *I see my life as full. I look for the value in every experience.*

- *I always acknowledge the good things and happy experiences I have in my life.*

- *I'm valuable and special just as I am. I don't need a relationship or anything else to determine my value.*

- *I'm a whole and complete person in and of myself. I'm not missing anything I need.*

- *I define myself; I don't need anyone else to define me.*

- *I'm secure within myself. I'm resourceful and capable in any situation.*

These beliefs resonate with a healthy magnetism that can only attract healthy, loving, treatment to you. A willingness to embrace these new, loving, and valuing mentalities opens your heart to the truest experience of love—one that isn't based in lack, and won't result in a relationship that lacks love.

Such new constructs are absolutely necessary to form the greater network of beliefs that will allow you to release urgency and transform your personal energy. In addition to how they positively impact your relationships, these new ideas are the source of the self-honoring attitudes that will enrich your life. Here are some affirmations to support your new approach.

Affirmations of Value

- *I take responsibility for my own happiness. I find things to be happy about every single day.*

- *I create a spirit of self-reliance and self-fulfillment in my daily life. I look upon all relationships as ways to enhance my life, not define it.*

- *My chosen perceptions are the real source of my happiness. I choose to perceive my life with love and appreciation.*

- *I take responsibility for my feelings and needs. I take action in my own behalf.*

- *I seek authentic power from within. I release the need to control or acquire.*

- *I seek acceptance of myself from within, not acceptance through the approval of others.*

- *I believe in myself; I value my integrity and my worth.*

- *I create balance in my life. I create joy, happiness, and many smiles a day.*

- *I'm strong, honest, confident, and forthcoming.*

- *I enjoy the present and trust in the future. I enjoy and acknowledge all that I have and do.*

- *I create my own destiny.*

- *I'm all that I need. I rely on myself. I love my loving energy!*

Repeat these new truths and others like them often. You have no idea what kind of hold your old constructs have on you—and the power they have to block your desires. It's time to let them go. In addition to letting go of the beliefs, you must also change the behaviors they support. *Stop looking for everything that is wrong. Stop the chronic complaining, and start acknowledging all that you have to be grateful for. Develop an awareness of what's truly valuable in your life. Express your appreciation often.*

Value is your soul's true legacy. Your choice to acknowledge life's value in every moment will liberate you from desperation. It will make every desire pure—and every intention healthy.

The Marriage of Desire and Intent

*"Whatever forces it, spoils it.
Whoever grasps it, loses it."*
— Lao Tzu

Your desires will be mere clouds in the wind if they're not supported by your intentions. If you don't want your yearning for love to drift away, you must *bring your intention to it.* You must *intend love*—not power, control, security, or approval—just love.

When a desire is pure, not laced with fear, it's based on an intention to *enhance, not define* your life. What you desire becomes more available to you, and your efforts to bring it about become more creative and dynamic. You can make sure your desire remains pure by following the four steps that will best engage the forces of the Universal Laws.

1. Define Yourself

All experiences are filtered through your self-definition. All of your happiness—and most of your misery—is based upon how you perceive and identify yourself. Your self-definition creates the very texture of your life, determining if you are likely to be happy or discontent, carefree or worrisome.

It's a good idea to pursue the process of self-definition in writing. Even if you already feel that you're in touch with how you perceive yourself, it would be very helpful to explore that now. For instance, take some time to establish for yourself who you are and where you came from. Disregard the mundane statistics such as "female from Ohio" or "teacher from Texas." Focus instead on the fundamental truth that preexisted your job, your earthly location, or even your gender.

A healthy definition of yourself starts with an essentially spiritual foundation. Even if you've never defined yourself in this way, or if it feels very foreign to you, consider it now. This is of primary importance, so open yourself up to a substantial awareness of your spiritual nature. It's infinite and resourceful, a compelling reason for you to feel confident and courageous in your pursuit of love.

> *Your spirit is blessed by the breath of the Divine. God's unconditional love gives you every reason to know that you're valuable, worthy, and deserving. This is the basis of all healthy pursuits—to define yourself in such a deep experience of God's love that no pursuit is really necessary. You are full, complete, and vibrant in this state, and all that you seek is desirable and available, but never necessary to define you.*

This kind of profound personal self-definition needs to be established in thought and reinforced in experience. Don't relegate it to an abstract concept, but actually form the words and statements that will create your personal truth. Meditate on your new definition. *Experience that truth in your heart and in your essence.*

You must redefine yourself fully, spiritually, and lovingly. If you don't, you'll be *compelled* to seek your definition from outside of yourself, often through your relationships. Looking for a relationship to light the darkness of your life is like looking in the distance for the switch to turn on your lights at home.

2. Take Responsibility for Yourself and Your Happiness

The process of redefining yourself establishes your eternal value and authentic power. Based on this, you must assume 100 percent responsibility for the *quality* of your life experience. You must first do this by pursuing interests of value and engaging in activities of honor and compassion. *If something is inherently unhealthy or harmful in your life, you must take responsibility for changing it.*

This decision to take responsibility marks a major shift in your personal energy. The energy of one who is decisive, self-directed, and responsible creates a harmonic resonance with the loving intention of the Universe. The energy of one who is undirected, reactionary, and irresponsible creates a vacuum where the loving intention of the Universe can't flourish.

> *Ultimately, no one else can assume responsibility for your identity, worth, or happiness. It is simply not possible to be so disempowered and still be happy! You have only two choices: to take responsibility for your own happiness, or be willing to be unhappy.*

Taking responsibility means refusing to be a passive witness to your life, always following the path of least resistance. It means asking yourself what *you* can do to *create* happiness, then putting forth the effort to do it. It means living with a purpose that's self-realized, asking the hard questions, and being accountable for the answers.

You don't need someone else to make you feel better about yourself. You don't need a relationship in order to be spontaneous, fun-loving, adventurous, or playful. Taking responsibility is the intent to actively bring these elements into your life *yourself*. It's choosing to see the potential for pleasure and peace in every moment, and to be optimistic, conscious, present, and aware. Continue making the choice to be happy. Perceive the joy that your daily life has to offer and create more of it. It's your responsibility!

3. Maintain Your Autonomy

Taking personal responsibility for yourself is important because it's the source of your *autonomy*. Autonomy is a celebration of one's individuality. An autonomous person demonstrates an independent spirit—even when in a relationship. Maintaining your independence is absolutely *essential* in resisting codependency and the energies of paradoxical intent.

Engaging in a successful relationship requires a delicate balance, a combination of *in*dependence and *inter*dependence. Ultimately, both parties are responsible for themselves, yet there's a sharing of responsibility for the relationship. There's also an active concern for the both partners' happiness and well-being. Maintaining your autonomy allows you to fully engage in this concern without sacrificing yourself or your identity.

Always embrace your own individual purpose. It's important to have something that you feel passionate about outside of the relationship. Set boundaries, even within the relationship. Put aside some time and space to pursue your purpose. Remember to maintain your own identity, for it's very easy to lose yourself in the status quo of a relationship. People tell me, "I used to listen to music. I used to go to plays. Now, all we do is watch television." Don't abandon what you enjoy—if your partner won't do these things with you, do them alone or with a friend. Taking responsibility includes honoring your own path.

Autonomy is necessary for a greater sense of control and balance in your relationship. Taking responsibility for yourself may be difficult because you have no one else to blame for not getting what you want out of life. But once you set aside this blame and start taking action, you'll be amazed at the power it creates! The real power to make your dreams come true lies in your own hands. Don't give that power away by making someone else responsible for you.

4. Be Optimistic

Of all of the seven types of toxic thinking discussed in Chapter 4, catastrophizing is the surest way to stimulate the negative energies of the Law of Paradoxical Intent. If you want to make your intention pure, *you must become more optimistic*. Being fearful and worrisome about what may or may not happen extends the assumption of lack out of the present and projects it into the unknown future, expanding this negative focus indefinitely. It will be very important, therefore, to be careful not to sabotage your magnetic energies with such catastrophic worries as:

- "What if I never get married?"

- "What if nobody ever asks me out?"

- "What if I'm always alone?"

- "The world is full of losers. What if I never find anyone who will treat me well?"

- "The world is cruel. What if I never get what I want?"

These catastrophic assumptions have no place in the energy of pure desire. They bring urgency to your intent and turn desire into desperation. Your fearful energy will inevitably turn people off and push them away, creating the very catastrophe you were worrying about.

No matter how convinced you may be that these catastrophic thoughts are true, this kind of thinking must be stopped. You must replace each thought with a much more optimistic assumption. Change every negative "what if" to the opposite, positive response, such as:

- "What if I *do* get asked out?"

- "What if I *do* succeed?

- "What if I *do* find a good relationship?"

- "What if I *could* get what I want?"

- "What if I *could* be happy now?"

In addition to these new "what ifs," you must *visualize* yourself engaging in those optimistic outcomes. Whatever it is you feel may *not* happen, visualize it happening. Picture yourself meeting someone wonderful, and imagine yourself going out on that first date. Visualize yourself being treated kindly and with respect. See yourself walking down the aisle and getting married. *Feel* how it would feel, and *know* that it's possible.

Envision it all, then release this picture out into the Universe with trust. Determine to create the loving and optimistic energy that will cause the laws to work in your favor. Even now they are helping to energize the cosmic forces that will make your dreams come true.

Love and companionship are waiting for you. Whether you're in a relationship or looking for one, your choice to focus on love instead of lack will enrich the value of every one of your life experiences. The Universe can't help but positively respond to your choice of a loving perception.

PART III

The Law of Harmony

*"Spirit is ever seeking
to draw back the many into the One."*
— Paramahansa Yogananda

Harmony is the beautiful resonance of peaceful energies and healthy intentions coming together. When we're in harmony with ourselves and others, it creates a fluidity to our life, a synchronicity that seems like coincidence but is really the spark of connecting consciousness.

The beginning of harmony is balance. The energy of harmony is love—all-embracing, non-competitive love. And the intention of harmony is reverence.

There's no higher vibrational frequency than the harmonic intention to bring reverence to ourselves and all we encounter. This intention not only changes our own destiny, but creates a shift in the Universal consciousness itself! This consciousness of reverence is the opus of the human heart.

❧ Chapter Twelve ❧

Playing in Harmony

*"Joy is the realization of oneness,
the oneness of our soul with the world,
and of the world-soul with the supreme love."*
— Rabindranath Tagore

There's a rhythm to the Universe that is an inexorable part of who you are. If you sit quietly, you can feel that rhythm moving through and around you, like the percussion within a symphony.

Whether or not each of us is in harmony with this Universal symphony depends on how we resonate with the energetic laws. As we've seen, the resonance of our personal energy determines what we magnetize, and the resonance of our intention determines the potential fulfillment of our desires. In both of these cases, the reverberations are internal. The third law, the **Law of Harmony,** not only responds to our internal vibrations, but it reacts to our energetic connections with the outside world as well.

The harmony that echoes throughout the world is in syncopation with the energy of Divine Love. It's an ever-present flow of potential. To the degree that we engage in loving connections with others, we either align with this rhythm or resist it. As we make harmonic choices in our dealings with others, we resonate with the magical frequency of the Universe that attracts more positive energies to our lives. There's a special presence when one is in harmony, a state of flow, a synchronicity that brings all of the elements of our life into alignment.

Being in rhythm with the Universe creates a shower of blessings, from the little unexpected surprises of daily life to the successful fulfillment of lifelong dreams. In harmony, we tend to have more energy, greater intuition, and a stronger sense of peace. And as more and more people create harmony *within* themselves, they increase the harmony *between* themselves, exciting a positive power that moves out to all people everywhere.

Our Entangled Web

There's a connectedness within the world, one that transcends the limited connections of friendship, family, nationality, or race. It's an interconnectedness that spans time and distance, differences and similarities. It's an energetic and essential connection.

Waves and particles are forever moving and changing places. You may believe that you are one constant, whole identity, contained within the boundaries of your skin and self-definition, but this is an illusion. Quantum parts of you have moved through time from distant places in the Universe, and they will move on again, reorganizing themselves, becoming someone or something else. In quantum reality, you're as much a process as you are a person!

One of the many interesting phenomena of quantum movement is called *phase entanglement,* the effect of the passage of one quantum entity on another. As the waves of two entities converge, they become "phase entangled," and each leaves some of its own properties with the other. This exchange of properties is then maintained even after the entities have parted.

It is, in part, this phenomenon that connects us and makes the world an undivided wholeness. Particles come and go. They stay for a while and then move on. Waves meet and move together; and when they leave, each identity, each consciousness has changed from the experience. Applied to the field of human experience, this phenomenon explains a lot! We mingle our energies with the people that we're exposed to, literally taking some of their energy away and leaving some of ours with them.

Have you ever noticed how contagious feelings are? When you spend time with someone who's depressed, you can actually notice yourself catching their feeling. Even if you're not conscious of it, you carry their energy with you in your own resonance. If you're exposed to a nervous person, their agitation stays with you, too. For this reason, it's important to be very discriminating about the people you surround yourself with. If someone's energy is bothering you, you must reduce your exposure to them. Set boundaries and investigate the relationship to discern what type of energy it's bringing to your life. Also develop an awareness of the energy you yourself are projecting, for it stimulates a great deal in your experience of others.

> *In our dealings with others, there are two main energies that impact our activation of the Law of Harmony. These are conflict and reverence. The flow of Harmony within our life is manifested in direct proportion to the absence of conflict there. Conflict, whether internal or external, creates a resistence to the natural rhythm of Universal energy. All conflict comes from the inability to experience reverence, whether it be reverence for self or for others.*

Reverence for self is our real source of harmony. Without it, we're plagued by worries and doubts; we're driven by feelings of inadequacy, constantly striving to gain from the outside that sense of approval that's missing within. This internal emptiness creates a frantic search for power that usually manifests itself in one of two ways. Some people grow passive and fearful, becoming people pleasers, seeking their power in the acceptance and reassurance of others. Others become aggressive, maybe even hostile, trying to force recognition and compliance from the rest of the world.

Without self-reverence, everything becomes secondary to the constant need that people have to feel good about themselves. Inevitably, everyone and everything is filtered through this issue. People are viewed either as the tools that could make good things happen or the obstacles that could take good feelings away. This kind of mentality leads to a range of difficult emotions, including fear, arrogance, anxiety, addictions, rage, depression, and even violence.

This is the energy of conflict—to use others, either passively or aggressively, in order to satisfy your longing for recognition. It stems from a void of reverence for yourself, and it makes you incapable of having reverence for the people you seek to manipulate. If you want to achieve real harmony—which is a pivotal piece in the puzzle of attraction—you need to examine how this kind of conflict plays itself out in your own nature and in your relationships with others.

Your Theory of Relativity

Where do you think you fall on the conflict/reverence scale? The answer can be found in how you see yourself in relation to other people. All of your relationships, including your romances, reflect one of your most fundamental beliefs. It's one of three basic beliefs that indicate both your attitude toward yourself and your aptitude for connecting with other people.

Although most people never speak it, and perhaps never realize it, everyone engages in one of three beliefs concerning how they see themselves relative to other people. Their surface attitudes may change according to the time, place, or company they keep, but the fundamental belief is what they filter most of their life—and all of their energy—through! In their most simple form, these beliefs are:

- *I'm inferior to others.*
- *I'm equal to others.*
- *I'm superior to others.*

In which of these three categories would you place yourself? You may not have consciously thought in these terms before, but now it's time to look at your deepest feelings. Look at the people in your life and in your world. How do you feel about them? How do you feel about yourself when you're with them?

Be honest with yourself—even if it's painful or embarrassing. If you're not immediately aware of the category that's most true for you, consider the following viewpoints. Which of these attitudes most adequately represents how you feel?

1. Deep down inside, I would have to say that I feel inferior to others. For the most part, I do see people as being better than me. The problem is that I'm not as confident (smart, strong, disciplined, courageous, or attractive) as most people I know.

2. I pretty much see myself as equal to other people. Our circumstances may be different, but really we're all the same. I know that every person is special in his or her own way. I like to look for the good in others as well as in myself.

3. If I had to be really honest, I would have to admit that I often see myself as superior to

others. It may sound proud, but I feel that
there are valid reasons why I should think so
highly of myself. I look around me and see
people who don't take responsibility, don't
make the grade. Why shouldn't I feel superior?

So, which is it? Do you see yourself as inferior, equal, or
superior? Or do you jump from one extreme to the other,
never really landing in the middle? Your answer is important,
since it's the basis for your self-perception, the ultimate
source of all your intentions.

A sense of inferiority doesn't always manifest in the
form of some simpering wimp, ready to let anybody walk all
over them. In fact, an inner sense of inferiority is often
masked by attitudes that look like superiority, even
arrogance. Don't let the bravado of superiority misguide
you about this—even if it's your own. Just as a large, beautiful house can be built on a sinkhole in the ground, a
strong, even overwhelming personality can be built on a
sinkhole of self-esteem.

Whether it comes from a need to compensate for what's
lacking, or just from a misinformed upbringing, feelings of
superiority are just as toxic as feelings of inferiority. Almost
every type of emotional discomfort, psychological anguish,
and relationship problem can be traced to the mental traps
of inferior or superior thinking. I call this *relative valuing*,
and it's based in the ego. It is a far different process than
intrinsic valuing, which comes from the heart.

Let Go of My Ego!

The word ego has had many different meanings. It originally meant the self, but lately it's developed a very bad rep-
utation. Now it usually refers to people who are self-centered,
self-serving, or conceited.

The ego is the part of us that wants us to establish ourselves as a priority. It's motivated to reach out for that which we haven't yet established in our own hearts—it's looking for a sense of safety and satisfaction with being who we are. The basic function of the ego is judgment and value assignment. The ego looks at the world only in terms of analyzing our place in it. It encourages us to judge others in order to feel better about ourselves. It forces us to judge ourselves whenever we've failed to measure up. For this reason, it becomes very difficult to experience the world through mere observation.

We observe all of the time. We look at ourselves, our environment, and other people, and we take notice of things. We notice things such as "My hair is turning gray," "Beth has gained some weight," or "Bob has a new car." All of these are simple observations that, taken as they are, don't have to have any emotional charge to them. Left as observations, all of these statements are safe for us and could remain so.

But the ego isn't satisfied with that—it wants to know where *we* stand in relation to all of this, to determine our value relative to the rest of the world. It doesn't want to stop with observation because merely observing doesn't promote power, control, or self-satisfaction. In this effort, it tends to change our observations into judgments, in order to make us feel better about ourselves. Unfortunately, its judgment isn't restricted to others, so it often makes us feel worse.

The observation "My hair is turning gray," then turns into a judgment about our age, which has the power to make us feel bad about ourselves. Beth gaining weight, turned into a judgment, could make us feel better about ourselves, while Bob buying a new car could make us feel worse. It's crazy, but this habit of judging creates an ever-present competition in which we're constantly racking up points either for or against the ego. Why should Beth gaining weight make us feel better? Why should Bob buying a new car make us feel worse? For that matter, why should graying hair make us feel bad?

After all, it's part of the natural process of life. Unfortunately, our modern culture has actually turned graying hair into a fault! And the ego screams at us to get rid of our faults. The fact is, no matter what else you may have already achieved, there's still at least one highly valued commodity that doesn't get better with age, and that is youth.

> *Stop comparing. There will always be people who are better off and people who are worse off. Whether it's about looks, money, happiness, success, or love, any comparison is an energy killer. Yet feeling equal— that is, truly seeing your inherent equality—stops the need to strive and prove. It creates a peaceful percep- tion that pervades your life and your energy with vibrations of love.*

Whatever they are, our comparisons to others draw out our feelings of inferiority or superiority. They create a roller-coaster ride of emotions. We may be up one day and down the next. As long as we're looking outside of ourselves, there *will always be* something for the ego to either condemn or applaud.

The ego's job is to secure superiority. It has a need to be extraordinary, to be special, to have more. It's a compulsion that comes from the sense of something missing within. And it's the ego's need to compensate for what seems to be miss- ing that creates the nagging voice of worry, fear, and criti- cism ever-present in our heads.

What the ego is actually seeking is love. But we can never attain that through worry, comparison, or judgment. In fact, paradoxical to our ego's intent, these are the very things that push love away. Love seeks to expand at every point, especially those points of greatest need—the empty hearts, the lonely souls, even our own frightened ego. When we stop compar- ing ourselves to others and competing with the rest of the world, we move out of the analysis of the mind and into the feelings of the heart, where we finally find our intrinsic value.

When we embrace the ego with love, we'll give it the energy it's seeking. It will no longer need to manipulate, compare, or judge to feel good, because it will be basking in the peace of our choice of self-acceptance. In fact, this is the *only* way to move out of the negative energies of both inferiority and superiority—and into the harmonic energies of seeing ourselves as *equal*.

Getting to I-Level

Equality—the genuine feeling of it—is the only way to tap in to the wonderful powers of the Law of Harmony. It moves us into a current that joins us with all of the wonderful people and positive energies the Universe has to offer. No matter what you've believed in the past, *you are equal,* and so is everyone else.

Your being equal is already established; don't delude yourself about this! This is a constant, so it's important to know that your *feeling* equal is what makes the difference in your energy. The Law of Harmony demands that you match your *feeling* with your *being*. Once again the Universal Laws reflect a fundamental quantum physical principle: Consciousness creates the reality; observation determines the event. What a fantastically liberating realization!

> *Where the Law of Harmony is concerned, it's our consciousness of our equality that determines how we connect with people. When we embrace the equality of all people, including ourselves, we move into the harmonic resonance which connects us with the right people at just the right time in amazingly productive, even miraculous, ways.*

It's only our attitude which can block this connection. We can never be conscious of our equality to others if we're focused on our feelings of inferiority. And we certainly can't be conscious of our equality if we're filled with grandiose ideas of our superiority, for each of these attitudes is a loss of integrity. The inferior mentality perpetuates a lie about ourself, while the superior mentality perpetuates a lie about others. This not only steeps us in negative energy, it magnetizes other people to us who are equally deceived.

Being In-fear-ior

Both feelings of inferiority and superiority can be traced back to how one was treated in childhood. Children who grow up suffering a lot of criticism, excessive demands, or the absence of genuine affection are made to believe that there's something wrong with them. Some people believe that conclusion and carry it with them into adulthood, living their entire lives with feelings of unworthiness and inferiority.

Other people fear that conclusion, and desperately try to cover it up. They spend their entire lives trying to prove their excellence. These people actually feel inferior but behave in ways that are intended to convince themselves and others of their superiority. They've been treated the same way, but learn to overcompensate—often engaging in arrogance, sarcasm, and bragging to impress others and to prove to themselves that the criticism or indifference of their childhood wasn't warranted.

Some people might think that having an attitude of superiority would be a plus where the laws of attraction are concerned. After all, the Law of Magnetism says we attract what we put out. One might conclude then that it would be a good thing to put out the energy of superiority. While it's always good to project the energy of confidence, an attitude of superiority is only masked inferiority, an underlying *lack* of confidence, which is the real resonant source.

Once again, the Universal Laws don't rely on the *appearance* of something to determine their responses—it's the underlying energetic truths that the Universal Laws respond to. People who sincerely believe that they're superior aren't only creating negative energy, they're deluding themselves.

The Tide of Entitlement

What passes for superiority are feelings of *entitlement*, which cause people to believe they actually do *deserve* more. The word *entitlement* originally referred to privileges given the titled nobility of Europe—it has nothing to do with deserving. This difference is very important. *Entitlement* comes from external conditions, *deserving* from an internal connection with your true intrinsic value. Entitlement often comes from an accident of birth, being born into the "right" family, the "right" money, the "right" religion, the "right" race. Deserving comes from your eternal and Divine heritage.

An attitude of entitlement dishonors you, implying you're valueless without these external conditions. It disempowers you because you look to your entitlement, not your spirit, as the source of your happiness!

An interesting and relatively recent take on this issue is establishing entitlement through lack, envy, and victimization. This is such a skewed sense of "deserving," it's frightening! It manifests in attitudes such as, "I deserve money because I'm poor," or "I deserve those tennis shoes because someone else has them." You *do* deserve money, those tennis shoes, or anything else you want—not because you're poor or rich, but because you're valuable! But your value is separate from external lack or privilege. You deserve nice things because the Universe is abundant and you have the right—and the responsibility—to make your own dreams come true.

This new type of entitlement is a weird mixture of inferiority and superiority, saying, "I'm less than others, so I deserve to be treated better." It creates an "owe me" approach to life: *My family owes me. The government owes me. The world owes me.* In its worst case: *Everyone but me is responsible for me.* Such approaches to life are completely disempowering. They tell us that we're not capable of creating what we want, and so we must turn to some other source, often an unwilling one, to create it for us.

Both "inferior" and "superior" attitudes of entitlement destroy your sense of intrinsic worth. They assign your power to externals and attribute your value to degrees of money or status. This blocks your harmonic connection and sabotages your goals. As a result, any intention to be entitled *must* be replaced by deserving and equality.

If you catch yourself engaging in words or behaviors to try to demonstrate superiority, be aware of the real energy you're projecting. What your behaviors really indicate is *need.* People who are truly self-accepting don't need to behave in any superior way. They do not need to brag about or flaunt their accomplishments—and they don't need to have power over people, rage at them, manipulate or belittle them.

Some people use criticism and sarcasm as a way to look good in front of others, never realizing that it has the opposite effect. Remember the Law of Paradoxical Intent: Your intention to prove your superiority through rude or controlling behaviors actually disgusts and alienates people, even if they don't reveal that to you.

If you feel a sense of inferiority, you absolutely *must* change that consciousness. Without self-love, the ego will constantly be at a loss. At best, it will be confused and searching, always feeling off balance and at odds with life. At worst, it will be resentful and defensive, perceiving every other person as a potential threat to its hoped-for safety, power, or peace. The only solution is to affirm and redefine your value in order to project a genuine energy of confidence.

Real confidence is a peaceful yet certain presence. It gives one the power to take care of oneself without needing to take control over others. People who are truly confident project a very relaxed energy. They're not agitated and powerless out of feeling inferior, and they're not agitating and power-mongering out of needing to be superior. Confidence and authentic power come from a heartfelt sense of one's personal equality and a recognition of the equality of every living being.

You'll always project your strongest self-perception outward. If you see fear and lack within, the world will be a lonely and hostile place. If you see value within, the world will be a treasure trove of joyous experiences. You can only see in the world that which you see in yourself.

The Characteristics of Equality

An attitude of equality is born out of a profound recognition of your own self worth with an equal acknowledgment of the worth of others. In this state, you're never powerless, and you never need to be falsely empowered. You are *self*-empowered, and you're delighted by the thought that others are empowered, too.

People who feel equal are aware of their power because they know that it comes from their spirit, their sacred source of origin. This connection with the Divine source is the seed of the most magnetic energy possible—the energy of reverence.

Reverence is the most stimulating quality of the Law of Harmony. If you truly want to be in that magical place where the Universe is harmonized with your every wish, you must develop the art of reverence. This includes reverence for yourself, for others, and for your personal and global environment.

Reverence is the conscious acknowledgment and appreciation of the sacred origin of all people and things. *Reverence for the Divine* is the first order of business—it's that connection that helps you identify your own inherent specialness. Even if you falsely feel that you have no other reason to love yourself, knowing that you're a child of God gives you the most important reason of all.

Next is *self-reverence,* which is the source of your own peace of mind and your peaceful interaction with others. It liberates you from frantic striving and competition and engenders a peace of mind that's inexhaustible. Without self-reverence, both power and balance are lost. You're out of the sacred loop, distancing yourself from the ultimate power that's available in your own sacred identity. Instead of rhythm and flow, there's stagnation and resistance—the rest of the world keeps moving to a Divine resonance that gets further and further outside of your reach, causing you to grasp and strive even more.

Finally, *reverence for others* stimulates the Law of Harmony because it frees us from conflict. With reverence in our hearts, we can stop living in fear and judgment and let go of the need to accumulate and control. So much of our lives is spent in turmoil trying desperately to sustain our fragile network of fraudulent power from without. But looking at ourselves and others with reverence stops that struggle and makes the world our sanctuary.

Reverence also helps us to approach life with the three other qualities of equality—tolerance, acceptance, and compassion. These are the hallmarks of a life of reverence. An attitude of acceptance isn't compelled to devalue, dissect, or destroy. An attitude of tolerance is flexible and flowing, without the need to control. With tolerance and acceptance, we can focus on similarities instead of differences, and can open our hearts to compassion. We no longer need to force our agenda on others—we can be at peace with our own individuality and comfortable with the individuality of others.

This allows us to see our interconnectedness, which is the undiluted source of Universal blessings.

Quantum physics shows that all of life is connected. These connections—wave meeting wave, consciousness meeting consciousness—make up the harmonic workings of the Universe. It's this connectedness that causes our own resonance to blend with the natural movement and music of life. Only by becoming connected through tolerance and acceptance, not disconnected through judgment, can we move into this harmonic flow and partake in its bounty.

Change Your Energy Now

All reverence requires a relentless refusal to judge. Judgement of self creates internal conflict and takes away the acceptance we're looking for. Judgment of others sabotages our intent because we can't help but eventually place the same judgments and conditions upon ourselves. So changing our patterns of judgment must become a top priority if we want to tap into the magic of Universal harmony.

Judgment of others sets us apart—instead of empowering us, our criticism only disenfranchises us. We must aggressively intervene on our critical tendencies, and see past the surface in everyone, not just in those we approve of.

We never reach our goals alone. In some way, we are always assisted by others. Being disenfranchised puts us at cross purposes, cutting us off from potentially helpful connections. To the extent that we engage in judgment, we further our energetic isolation. But there's one very powerful intention that moves us back into the Universal flow: compassion.

Compassion isn't only a refusal to judge, it's a determination to love—to live with sympathy, forgiveness, and understanding. A compassionate heart longs

*to engage in kindness and caring, not for any other
gain but for the sake of compassion itself. Your choice
to assist and share amplifies the harmonic vibration,
which then resonates through the Universe and brings
your loving compassion back to you.*

Of course it's important to remember that being sympathetic and compassionate isn't the same as being passive and submissive. Our sympathy and compassion must extend to ourselves, too, or it leads to feelings of inferiority, just as the lack of compassion for others generates feelings of superiority. Real compassion comes from a safe heart and a gentle, caring attitude.

This is what being in harmony is all about. There is a reciprocity of our energy, an exchange on our love. We give reverence to all that we see, and all that we see blesses us in return. Our intention to revere all things spreads waves of joy and fills our Universe with gratitude, and the Universe reciprocates, giving us a magical life—where our difficulties are resolved much more easily and our happiness is multiplied beyond our expectations. This is the State of Harmony—to find it you must be *equal* to the task.

❧ CHAPTER THIRTEEN ❧

Learning to Love

"When you commit to a spiritual relationship with another human being, you begin to see that what is necessary to the health of your partnership is identical with what is necessary to your own spiritual growth, that each of you holds the pieces that the other is missing."
— Gary Zukav

The elements of the Law of Harmony apply to *all* of your relationships. The resonance of how you connect with others goes a long way toward determining how smoothly your life flows. Since your love relationship is one of the most primary relationships of your life, it's also one of the strongest factors of your harmonic resonance in the world.

Healthy relationships are made up of relatively sound and responsible people who know that to make the connection work, they need to put forth some effort, prioritizing the other person and the partnership itself. In fact, pretty much any relationship is salvageable if both parties are willing to really work on it.

There are three things that are absolutely fundamental to any mutually nurturing relationship. This isn't limited to romantic relationships, but includes all of the significant associations of your life. I call them the Three R's: respect, reciprocity, and real communication. You may be able to maintain a connection without these ingredients, but don't kid yourself about having a real relationship.

1. Respect

When people come to me for relationship counseling, I start by asking them two questions: Do you respect your partner? Does your partner respect you? I start with these questions because if there's no respect on the part of one of the partners, it's very unlikely that person will be willing to do the work it takes to make the relationship better.

Believe it or not, almost everything else needed in a relationship can be taught if both people are willing to learn. If the relationship didn't start with respect, however, it was never really a relationship at all—it was entered into for the wrong reasons, and was intended as something else—probably acquisition, manipulation, or usery.

This is why I always tell my dating clients to *be very aware of any signs of disrespect.* I'm always amazed, however, at the amount of clients (especially women) who have been willing to disregard those signs. They think that the respect will get better once they're married. Never make that assumption! It's hard enough to maintain respect as time goes on, never mind having to establish it after the infatuation wears off. Trust me—been there, done that! There's nothing more lonely than to be in a relationship where you're not respected. Your time together is empty, filled with dread and apprehension.

So if you're one of those people who thinks that any relationship is better than no relationship at all, you'd better think twice. Not only does that thought dishonor you, but the Universe may just send you something to educate you on this matter.

Without respect in a relationship, someone is just being used. It's more of a service than a love partnership. This is why the feelings of emptiness are so great—you're looking to your relationship for a sense of support. Not only does that *not* happen when there's no respect, but the exact *opposite* happens and you sense a loss of support. And sooner or later, staying in a partnership where you're not respected will also cost you your own self-respect. Since self-honoring is virtually impossible when you consistently allow someone—especially your significant someone—to dishonor you, it can only attract more and more misery down the road.

There's no question that mutual respect is the foundation of any happy and strong relationship. All good things that come—including real depth of feeling and willingness to prioritize each other—come from a mutual reverence and regard for your loved one. This kind of respect can take the connection to incredible heights and make it a profoundly spiritual one. Yet without it, your relationship will turn into one struggle after another.

You're not taking the easy way out by choosing to stay in a relationship that's devoid of respect—in reality, that choice is the longest, hardest road you can travel. You deserve more, much more, such as knowing that you have the good opinion of your partner. You also deserve the sharing and caring that comes from equal partners prioritizing each other. In fact, the only way that you can achieve the kind of reciprocity that a healthy relationship calls for is to begin with mutual respect.

2. Reciprocity

Reciprocity is the balance within a relationship. It starts with the fundamental assumption by each person that you are *two equal partners*. From that assumption, based in mutual respect, the two of you form an *interdependent relationship*, which is a mutually nurturing and reliant lifestyle, utilizing each person's talents and abilities in order to make the relationship run smoothly. Responsibilities are shared; partners are willing to help each other—often agreeing on dividing up the tasks and taking on certain roles.

No one can tell two people what makes a relationship reciprocal. They can only decide that for themselves. But they need to talk about it honestly. They need to arrive at their agreement without coercion or manipulation. Compromise and flexibility are a must, especially when the needs of the relationship or its individuals change.

For instance, men and women tend to reciprocate in different ways. Domestic responsibilities and finances are two of the biggest issues that must be worked out, as women are working more, and many men are taking on more domestic responsibility, especially in the upbringing of their children. (Yet in spite of all this, most women will tell you that, job or no job, the bulk of the housework falls largely on their shoulders.) But sharing the *effort* of living and *making* a living is a part of the partnership. It may not be equal, but it must be shared. If it's not, the relating will soon turn into resenting. In fact, *without reciprocity, you no longer have a relationship. All you have is a habit!*

> *Emotional reciprocity is also a part of what makes a good relationship. This is the genuine sharing of feelings, opinions, and desires. In an emotionally reciprocal relationship, the partners encourage and support each other. There's a relaxed environment, one in which each partner is comfortable discussing his or her problems without fear of being ignored or judged.*

This is so intrinsic to a healthy relationship that it cannot be overemphasized. Without emotional reciprocity in their romantic relationship, a person feels minimized and disconnected. This is isolating at best and seriously traumatizing at worst—if it continues for any length of time, it can result in the destruction of one's self-esteem. It certainly results in destroying the relationship, even if some connection is maintained. This is a devastatingly lonely place to be, and you never want to go there if you can possibly help it.

The absence of reciprocity starts with a lack of respect, and it takes self-respect to get the reciprocity back. While nothing is ever really 50/50, and no two people ever give equal amounts of all things in any relationship, a strong sense of reciprocity can be achieved. It comes from sharing effort, time, and responsibilities. Each person must consider—and try to honor—what the other person needs. Reciprocity requires balance—and the willingness to communicate about what it takes to make that balance work.

3. Real Communication

The third ingredient that's necessary for a healthy relationship is *real* communication. You simply can't relate without communicating. In fact, a relationship without communication reduces your partner to merely your roommate. Even if you only consider the sexual aspect of this, sex with an acquaintance feels pretty empty indeed. That's just the tip of the iceberg where lack of communication is concerned, and it's a big enough iceberg to sink the relation*ship!*

There are three basic types of communication, with many variations thereof. The first is *superficial communication*—discussing the weather, sports scores, and the latest movies. The next is *logistical communication,* covering questions about what to have for dinner, what bills need to be paid, and where to go on vacation. Finally, there's *intimate communication,* which includes both emotional and sexual intimacy. These are expressions of feelings, fears, and desires; and discussions of problems, needs, and concerns. Intimate talk can cover everything from the boss who makes you crazy at work to what makes you excited in bed. *Real* communication includes all three of these—superficial, logistical, and especially intimate communication.

Superficial communication is fairly easy for most people, since we do it all the time. It may get us through the day and help us deal with acquaintances, but it's certainly not enough to make a relationship real. Logistical communication is also pretty easy, as it's generally task oriented and therefore usually doesn't cause people to feel vulnerable.

The most difficult type of commination for most people is the intimate variety. The expression of one's deepest feelings can be very risky. More people are actually willing to take this risk at the beginning of the relationship, probably because they feel their partner will be more supportive at this tender point. Over time, however, if they're not truly accustomed to revealing themselves in this way, they're likely to shut this part of themselves down, resorting to superficial and logistical communication as their major form of connecting. Yet even these relationships aren't without hope— real communication is a skill that *can* be learned.

To communicate actively, you need to engage in four activities: talking, listening, hearing, and responding. This may seem basic, but you'd be surprised by how many people stop at step one or two. In the process of real communication, each party *interacts* with the other. Party One speaks about something. Party Two listens, *hears it,* and then *actively responds*— with an opinion, some encouragement, or an emotional or personal reaction. The response allows the communication to build. Without the response, it's not communication, but mere dissemination of information.

As speakers, we need to say *what we mean* in a tone of voice that's nonthreatening. Listeners need to *hear* what's being said and respond appropriately. Sometimes the response will call for a personal reaction, an expression of our own experiences, feelings, or opinions; sometimes all that's needed is a sympathetic reaction. Other times we may feel the need to ask questions, gain clarity, or get more information. Our response shows our interest—it's how we relate and forge our connections.

Lack of communication is the biggest complaint I see in my relationship counseling. This is probably due to the fact that men and women have such different styles of communicating. While women can often be very emotional in their communication, many men have been trained from early on to hide their emotions. This polar kind of approach can create a lot of problems: Men don't want to deal with the "drama," and women can't understand why communicating is so hard.

People have to *learn how to communicate* with each other. It begins by creating a safe and comfortable environment. Set aside time to talk. Really hear what your partner is saying. Be open and patient. It may feel awkward at first, but have the courage to stay with it. Real communication is absolutely crucial in maintaining the life of the relationship. It's part of what we should be able to expect from love.

Reasonable Expectations

Assuming that respect, reciprocity, and real communication are well in place, there are some other qualities that a healthy relationship should be able to offer. Although you're the first one responsible for your own happiness, it's reasonable to expect your relationship to contribute to that happiness. After all, the very reason two people pursue a relationship is because they're looking for a safe place with a compassionate partner. We want to go through life with someone knowing that we'll be supported, encouraged, and accepted—and knowing that we will bring the same support to our loved one in return.

So take a look at the following list. If you're unattached and programming for your future partner, start affirming that you're attracting a partner with the qualities that are most important to you. If you're in a relationship, look at the list together and talk about how you feel. Be honest, not judgmental. While no relationship is perfect, you should be able to expect some of these qualities at least some of the time.

1. Honesty, Integrity, and Trust

Honesty and trust are very closely related. You need to know that your partner has integrity, for if you see them lying to others, it won't take long before you assume that they're capable of lying to you. And if you can't be honest with each other, it will be impossible to foster an environment of trust.

Some people have a hard time trusting, not because their partner is untrustworthy, but because they themselves are *untrusting*. It's likely that they've been betrayed in the past. A person who is untrusting needs to look at the real source of their pain so that they don't have to project their own fears onto their partner. A person who is *untrustworthy* needs to look at how they use their deceitfulness to give them a false sense of power.

Honesty requires an openness about what's going on in each of your lives. You know what's important—and what needs to be disclosed. It may be difficult at times, but deceit is never an option. In a good relationship, partners use honesty to connect. They tell the truth, but they never use honesty as an excuse to be judgmental.

2. Acceptance, Tolerance, and Patience

Letting go of judgment is an important part of establishing mutual acceptance. In a healthy relationship, partners acknowledge each other's differences and learn to accept them. Nobody's perfect, and you need to tolerate each other's little quirks and idiosyncrasies.

Commitment is a statement of acceptance. It's a willingness to focus on the wonderful things that excite and entertain you about your partner, and to overlook the minor annoyances that every relationship carries. Short of your partner engaging in something dishonoring to you, your decision to commit to them means that you've decided to accept them as they are. You are committed to being patient, flexible, and forgiving. And since people change, accepting them as they are now means also accepting them as they will be tomorrow. You'll notice that the marriage vows don't say "Love and honor until one of us irritates the hell out of the other."

3. Appreciation, Encouragement, and Acknowledgment

Everyone needs to be appreciated. More than that, they need to be *told* that they're appreciated. They need to be acknowledged for who they are and what they do. And they need to be encouraged when the going gets rough. This isn't all that difficult to do, yet there are so many people who refuse to praise or compliment their spouses. This makes a huge difference in the experience of the relationship.

It's inestimably valuable to know that your loved one believes in you, acknowledges your efforts, and appreciates your special qualities. A peaceful harmony could be so easily achieved—and so much unity established—just by using some simple statements such as the following:

- "I know how hard you work, and I want you to know that I appreciate all your effort."

- "Did I ever tell you how much I respect you? I'm really proud of you!"

- "These are the things I love about you . . . "

- "I really appreciate it when . . . "

- "I believe in you. You can do anything you set your mind to."

These are wonderfully endearing ways to connect. They forge a depth of unity that enriches each person's life. Give them a try!

4. Presence and Priority

If you're going to make a relationship work, you'd better plan on *being present*, which means being there, both physically and emotionally. It means being available for companionship, conversation, and affection.

In our fast-paced world of two-career families, it's not uncommon for couples to see very little of each other from day to day and even from week to week. But you simply can't relate to someone if you're never together—in time, you'll look at your loved one and see a stranger. If you don't want this happening to you, you must prioritize each other and the relationship. It takes some planning, but you *can* have regular quality time together. You have to schedule it, and you have to make it *just as important* as your other priorities.

5. Flexibility and Freedom

Everyone needs at least some autonomy within their relationship. If each partner is to keep their own identity, it would require having the freedom to maintain their own interests. This requires balance. But if each of you is willing to be flexible and prioritize the other's needs, you should be able to help each other maintain the activities that you enjoy.

Flexibility is also necessary when approaching the daily demands of life. If you're too structured and inflexible, it indicates a subtle (or not so subtle) need for control. Since you can neither control life nor other people, needing to do so will only create conflict. A lot of little squabbles could be avoided if people would be just a little more flexible with each other.

6. Kindness and Affection

Affection is the tender and loving expression that creates a real communion between two souls. A touch, a kiss, a caress—all are little signs of affection. It only takes a moment to share a sweet sentiment.

> *Each little display of affection is like nourishment to the relationship. It feeds the connection. Each touch says, "I'm glad you're here." Each tender look or soft embrace says, "I would choose you all over again."*

Showing kindness is also a sign of affection. Assisting in some mundane task, giving a compliment, or a note of affection may be all your partner needs to get them through their day. It doesn't take much effort, but it creates so much harmony! Don't be threatened by it—kindness is more powerful than meanness. The mutual sense of support will help you thrive as individuals and bring you much closer as a couple.

7. Forgiveness

Human beings make mistakes. Even in the best relation-ships, they say hurtful things and behave selfishly at times. It would be virtually impossible in any long-term relationship to *never* offend or be offended by your partner. When that happens, "I'm sorry" not only needs to be said, it needs to be accepted. Without the ability and willingness to forgive each other, the little offenses would only mount up, creating a considerable bitterness, even if it were unspoken.

> *Forgiveness is both healing and liberating. A truly*
> *healthy person will see the power that comes from*
> *both asking for forgiveness and being willing to give it.*
> *There's a beautiful harmony that resonates between*
> *two people who are willing to talk things through,*
> *have compassion for each other, and release the need*
> *to be right all of the time.*

Forgiving each other for the little things shows flexibility and helps to build patience, tolerance, and acceptance. But the intention to forgive doesn't require you to submit to dishonoring treatment. When you're dealing with the big issues, you must make some important choices. You'll ultimately find, however, that honoring and forgiveness are the keys to moving the relationship from conflict to compassion.

❄❄❄

These are the qualities of healthy people and healthy relationships—but don't feel discouraged if your relationship is missing some. If your relationship is worthwhile, it's worth working on. Give it time. Keep up the communication. Never stop knowing that you deserve to be loved. This is the essence of the Law of Harmony at work in your relationship. Life is a process, and learning how to relate is a lifelong process. You need to grow and let go, learn and expand, make mistakes and forgive.

If you're looking for love, know that these qualities do indeed exist. There are many wonderful people who are looking for the same things. They want healthy relationships, and they're willing to work on them. The Universe is abundant—you *can* have the kind of mutually nurturing relationship you want. You should be able to expect open communication, respect, and acceptance. You should have—and be—the kind of partner who's present, compassionate, flexible, and kind.

> *To develop this kind of harmony with your partner, you must first bring real harmony to yourself. It's impossible to harmonize with anyone else if your own instrument is out of tune. Before you expect these qualities of your relationship, you must expect them of yourself.*
>
> *If you're looking for support in your relationship, you must start by supporting yourself. The same is true for forgiving, tolerating, accepting, and prioritizing yourself. Do you bring these wonderful intentions to your relationship with yourself? Be the partner you're looking for and you won't have to look for long.*

You are your own best source of support, encouragement, and compassion. If you can't expect this from yourself, you can't expect it from others—even significant others. In the absence of your own love and support, you'll only be desperate for it in your relationship. This could result in some very dangerous expectations.

Dangerous Expectations

Nobody can live up to impossible expectations. Nobody can impose them without becoming disappointed. If the following dangerous expectations are persisted in, the resulting resentment of one partner and the unfulfilled needs of the other will eventually drive the relationship into the ground. When the impossible is expected in a relationship, the relationship itself becomes impossible.

1. Don't Expect Your Partner to be Everything *to* You (or Give Up Everything *for* You)

It's utterly impossible for anyone to be all that you need. If you start with the realization that *you* are all that you need, it will never even occur to you to look for that in another. Nor should anyone be expected to give up all things for another. You and your partner are unique and need to stay that way. Expecting your partner to give up what makes them unique is the worst kind of emotional blackmail. In essence, you're saying, "I fell in love with who you are; now to keep my love, you must change that."

2. Never Expect Your Partner to Read Your Mind

People think that if they've been going together for a while, they should have some sort of unspoken connection. Not so! No one should have to anticipate your needs, even if you think those needs should be obvious. If you want to take a healthy responsibility for your part of the relationship, you should be willing to *ask* for what you need! I often hear people say things like, "If he loved me, he'd know what to say;" or "If she loved me, she'd know what to do." This is pure manipulation, resorted to in the place of honest and self-responsible communication. Express what you want or be willing to not get it!

3. Never Expect Your Partner to be Responsible for Your Happiness

A refusal to take responsibility for your happiness is a refusal to *be* happy. No matter how convinced you are that you can guilt-trip, coerce, browbeat, or otherwise force someone into taking responsibility for your happiness, it cannot and will not happen. *This attitude is second only to giving up your honor in the list of disempowering choices.*

Figure out what action you can take to create authentic happiness in your life, *then take it.* This is an absolute necessity for both your personal energy and your harmonic resonance. Giving someone else responsibility for your happiness will pretty much guarantee that you'll never have any.

4. Don't Assume That You and Your Partner Will Always Agree on Everything

No two people are alike—they have different opinions and approaches to life. While most things are relatively easy to negotiate, others may not be so easy. When two people differ on the major questions in life, it could create some conflict. But with communication and compromise, you should be able to work things out.

In processing a problem, first agree that each person has the right to their opinion. Never judge or attack each other for those differing opinions. Try to create some balance and arrive at a middle approach. There are questions each of you can ask yourself to help remedy the situation—as well as maintain the goodwill between you:

- *How would I want to be treated in this situation?*

- *How can I express my opinions or feelings calmly and with respect?*

- *Am I really honoring myself and my partner in the way I'm dealing with this issue?*

- *What can we do together to arrive at a balanced solution?*

Asking yourselves these questions—and really trying to implement their solutions—will go a long way in making your relationship more harmonious. With respect, reciprocity, and real communication you should be able to handle anything.

Change Your Energy Now

Take the risk of extending yourself. Truly be there for each other. If you're waiting for a relationship, truly be there for yourself. Look for opportunities to be tender and encouraging, and try to be more present by listening, noticing, loving. It isn't work, it's the intention of creating a loving relationship, an intention that will return great joy.

I often think that if people took care of their houses the same way they took care of their relationships, they would soon be coming home to a dirty, dilapidated mess. Then they'd wonder why it was so depressing to come home! Your relationship maintenance deserves *at least as much effort* as your house maintenance does. Still, people are willing to spend hours cleaning or doing yard work without giving more than a few passing moments to maintaining their love.

Try this: Figure out how much time you spend each week on laundry, mowing the lawn, or performing your other household tasks, and then spend *at least* that much time each week with each other, working on the relationship. Get to know each other again. Express your hopes and dreams. Talk about what you appreciate in each other. Discuss where you want to be in ten years, both individually and as a couple. If you're going to spend all those years (and more) together, don't just make it work, make it wonderful!

❧ CHAPTER FOURTEEN ❧

Sex and the Universal Laws

*"Her image had passed into his soul forever and
no word had broken the holy silence of his ecstasy."*
— James Joyce

Sex is a sacred thing. It's not just a primal need, although
many people see it that way. It's not just a bodily function, either, for a sexual connection can bring a relationship to truly profound levels of intimacy. It unites you
with your partner at a level of communication that can't be
achieved in any other manner.

The sexual experience is a wonderful exploration of
the most private feelings one person can have for another.
It's the sharing of passion blessed with trust, yet often filtered through at least a little vulnerability. When you think
of it, though, being open to that bit of vulnerability only
makes the experience that much more meaningful. This
wonderful connection—like everything else—is influenced
by the Universal Laws. Since sex is such an important relationship energy, it's well worth looking into how the laws
relate to it in detail.

Sex and the Law of Magnetism

The Law of Magnetism applies to your sexual, as well as personal, attraction. If you're single and want to magnetize a sexually intimate relationship, or if you're already in a relationship and desire a more active sex life, it might be helpful to consider the magnetic nature of your sexual energy.

Loving yourself and seeing yourself as sexy is the vibrational source of a sexually stimulating frequency. Being confident with yourself and your own sexuality, and knowing that you deserve an exciting sexual relationship, are critical factors in magnetizing one.

Since your beliefs are the resonant source of what you attract, it's very important to investigate what you believe about sex. So many people were told when they were young that sex is bad. Parents, religions, and cultures impose this belief as a way to control the behavior of their children. Some people, especially women, have even been given the archaic notion that sex should not be enjoyed. Such beliefs are fear-based, often causing people to resist the sexual experience entirely. Moreover, they split your intention, at once broadcasting that you desire romance, yet want to avoid sex. This can effectively block the opportunity of meeting someone who would like to have a fully intimate relationship with you.

Your beliefs about yourself and your sexuality are a significant part of your personal energy field, influencing the waves of sexual energy you're sending out. Here are some beliefs to consider—your true-or-false responses will indicate the kind of energy you're projecting concerning this issue.

Answer True or False:

1. I believe in myself and in my ability to be intimate in every way.

2. I see myself as a sexual person, and I accept myself that way.

3. I believe it's healthy for me to want sex.

4. I believe it's healthy for me to enjoy sex.

5. It's safe for me to be sexual with another.

6. I accept my body as it is now and am comfortable sharing it in a sexual way.

7. Sex is a healthy and natural way for two people to communicate their love.

8. I'm in control of my sexual life. I make honoring choices about my sexual activity.

If you answered *true* to five or more statements, then you're projecting a relatively healthy sexual energy and should be able to attract an intimate relationship—if your other energy sources are honoring. If you answered *false* to four or more, then you're very conflicted about your sexual desire.

Whatever your score, you need to work on the conclusions that you marked as *false*. Try to do some writing to get at the root of your feelings about them. Where did these thoughts come from? Can you recall how they might have originated? What do you really believe? What do you want to be true for you? Use each statement that you marked as *false* as a daily affirmation, and change any other toxic assumptions that you may have about sex. This will help to change your energy and support your intention to attract a relationship that's healthy and intimate on all levels.

Putting Away the Past

If you've been hurt in a past sexual relationship, you may need to ventilate some of your anger and frustration about that. Do a journal entry where you write a letter to the other person expressing all of your fears and feelings. Then reread that entry to discover any toxic conclusions you may have made about sex as a result of that experience.

It's not uncommon for us to make conclusions based on our pain. Unfortunately, these conclusions can affect the rest of our lives. If a difficult experience has caused you to decide, "I can't trust a sexual partner," this will either insulate you from attracting *any* partner at all, or it will magnetize a partner who is indeed untrustworthy where sex is concerned.

You need to do several thought sheets restructuring the unhealthy conclusions you may have made as a result of any traumatic sexual experience of the past. Use the restructured beliefs in the right-hand column as your own affirmations. Repeat them until you dispose of your difficult history.

If, somewhere along the way, you've been misinformed about sex—if you've been led to believe that sex is wrong, bad, unhealthy, or even unnecessary—you definitely need to address that. Having these beliefs firmly established in your energy could sabotage all of the other work you may be doing to magnetize a healthy romantic relationship. *An intimate relationship includes sex.* You can't project your intention for a romance and withhold your intention to have sex. The conflicting intentions will cancel each other out.

You need to create some affirmations that reverse your conflicting intentions. Add them to the statements above and to any others you may come up with in your self-investigation. All of your affirmations need to become true for you if you want to attract an intimate relationship—and have a healthy sex life once you get it.

If you're already in a relationship but aren't having the sexual experience you desire, it would be helpful for both you and your partner to respond to the above true-and-false statements. In addition, you have to look at what's going on in the rest of the relationship. The desire for sex is intrinsically connected to these factors. Finally, you should determine how you can increase the sensuality in your relationship.

The Realm of the Senses

Sex is one of the most highly sensual of all human experiences. Every one of the five senses is engaged during sexual interaction. If you want to increase your sexual energy, you have to increase the *sensual* energy in your life. The more you use, enjoy, and pay attention to your senses, the more you magnetize sensual and sexual experiences to you.

Even if your ultimate intention doesn't include magnetizing a more sexual relationship, being more sensual enhances all of your magnetic and harmonious energies, bringing many other blessings as well. The more you appreciate the joys of the senses, the more you'll attract pleasurable experiences to you, sexual or otherwise.

Consider each of the senses. Allow yourself to be open to new ideas that help expand your sensual experiences. Appreciating the joys of each sense activates other joyous consequences in your life.

Enjoy your sense of *touch*. Get a massage. Buy some satin sheets. (Don't make the mistake of believing that you have to be in a relationship before you can go to sleep in a soft, sensuous bed.) *Hear* with pleasure. Remember the power of acoustic energy. Listen to soothing, sensual music. Talk to yourself. Laugh a lot. Enjoy the sounds of nature, the song of the birds, the wind in the trees, even the beauty of silence—these are all gifts in the realm of the senses.

Surround yourself with wonderful scents. *Smell* the scents of the season: the damp aroma of freshly cut grass in summer, the spiciness of fallen pine needles in autumn, the wonderful incense of wood burning in the fireplace in the winter, the heavenly intoxication of spring flowers. You can also enjoy the sense of smell while you're experiencing the sense of *taste*. When you're eating, take the time to really notice the tastes. Savor every sweet, bitter, or spicy flavor. Don't just inhale your food; really appreciate it.

Finally, pay more attention to everything you *see*. Take the time to look at nature. See the grandeur of the sparkling stars on a charcoal sky, the color of the leaves in the trees. Allow yourself to see it all. Let each scene move into your feelings. By the same token, decorate with colors that are vibrant and energetic—or soft and soothing. Collect the kind of artwork that inspires you. Look for the beauty in your life. We're often surrounded with visually wonderful things but are in too much of a hurry to take the time to appreciate them!

You can combine all of these elements to make your home a very sensual environment. Place some wind chimes outside the bedroom windows. Play music more often than you watch television. Burn scented candles. Bake some cookies. Savor their wonderful smell floating through the house, then eat the cookies slowly, enjoying every bite.

All of these things will boost your energy of sensuality. At the very least, they'll make your life richer and more enjoyable. More than that, however, they resonate with a vibration that could help you magnetize the sensual relationship that you desire.

Sex and the Law of Pure Desire

Part of the desire for sex is fed by anticipation, starting with the excitement of the chase. Once the decision to date has been made, the physical arousal sets in. With the kissing, touching, and petting, the desire for sex builds to an almost irresistible point—leading to the ultimate culmination, what everyone is looking for in the sexual experience: the orgasm.

Technically speaking, the experience of orgasm—for both men and women—is well under a minute of sensation, consisting of eight spasms, each about a second long. When I tell this to my clients, they're utterly amazed.

"Is that all it is?" one of them responded. "Everyone makes all this fuss for just that?"

But of course the sexual relationship isn't just about that. It's the combination of all of the joys that such a relationship can bring to your life. For most people, it's the relationship and not just the sex that stimulates the desire for love. With that in mind, let's review just how the elements of the Law of Pure Desire specifically apply to the sexual relationship.

Hope for an intimate relationship can't be reduced to just a hope for sex. It's driven by a longing that's much more profound, a yearning for that deeply personal connection that feels like timeless recognition. For instance, when a friend of mine met the woman of his dreams, he was moved to tears, saying he'd finally felt like he found his way home after being lost forever. Hoping to find this kind of profound union is natural. We're all looking to establish the depth of connection that makes us feel we've finally "come home." What we're hoping for is an all-consuming resonance of heart, soul, and mind. And when we find it, we can't help but get excited.

If *excitement* is the emotional energizer of the Law of Pure Desire, it's certainly both the emotional and physical energy of the sexual experience. The chemistry of falling in love is compelling—emotions run high, as do hormones and endorphins. Serotonin levels increase when one is falling in love, creating a greater sense of well-being. Oxytocin, the "touch hormone," is introduced into the bloodstream every time affectionate physical contact is made—this drives up the desire for more touch and closeness and greater intimacy. Endorphins are released in the brain that act like stimulants. People experience loss of appetite, increased energy, and a much higher degree of optimism, all because of the chemical effects of falling in love.

It's easy to maintain sexual excitement in the early stages of the relationship. The novelty and chemistry combine to promote an ongoing sense of excitement. Over time, however, sexual routines become established, and people start to take sex for granted. Often, the sex itself becomes so predictable and unexciting that it doesn't even seem worth the time or effort. If this has happened to you, don't despair. You needn't either throw out the relationship or resign yourself to an uneventful or nonexistent sex life. There's a technique designed to address the loss of sexual interest and excitement called *sensate focusing.*

Sensate focusing is concerned with the senses, not the sex. For at least two weeks, the actual sexual intercourse is taken out of the picture. The couple spends at least 20 minutes a day sharing sensual stimulation without having sex. This is done by giving each other back rubs or whole-body massages. Try taking a bubble bath or shower together; wash each other's body and dry each other off. Take a soft feather and gently rub it up and down each other's naked body. Kiss, touch, and caress, but don't have sex.

Do this 20 minutes every day for two weeks. If boredom is the only problem, you should certainly be feeling renewed sexual interest by now. If something else is going on, you may be able to find the answer in the other elements of desire.

As we've seen, what you *believe* about sex will have a strong influence on your sexual desire. Your sexual pleasure is bound to be affected by whether or not you believe in your partner's love and respect for you. It's very difficult to let down your inhibitions and open yourself to the pure joy of the sexual experience if you're worried about being judged or dismissed. You *deserve* a relationship where the sex is good because the partnership is great. You deserve to be treated with respect in the bedroom, and to have your sexual needs met. But you must communicate openly about those needs and believe in your partner's willingness to satisfy them. There's power in your beliefs, and that power extends to your sexual experience. And it's equally influenced by the element of surrender.

The element of *surrender,* pertaining to the sexual side of your relationship, doesn't mean giving up sex. It means surrendering whatever *personal agenda* you may be attaching to it. Sex is the intimate, physical expression of mutual love. Defining it as *anything else* changes it to mere manipulation. Unfortunately, people often use their sex life to define themselves. Many people use sex to convince themselves of their own value. Some people see it as a source of power; others see it as evidence that they're still desirable.

> *You can't use sex as a way to prove anything about yourself, whether it be your power, value, or attractiveness. If you do, you'll be forcing your partner to take responsibility for your good feelings about yourself. This is a very dangerous approach. Your partner can't give you your self-esteem, your sense of being attractive, or your happiness—through sex or any other means.*

To impose such expectations is utterly catastrophic if you want to maintain a healthy and genuine relationship. If you find yourself doing this, you definitely need to investigate your intentions. Your intention to make someone responsible for you is a sure way to stop them from loving you.

Sex and the Law of Paradoxical Intent

Where your intention is concerned, sex is no different from any other goal or desire. If you're urgent about it—or if your intention isn't honoring—you'll invariably push that desire away. People enter into a sexual relationship for a lot of reasons—not all of them healthy—and they need to know why.

Some people see sex as a form of behavioral commitment, but unless other commitments have been made, it's no such thing. Many see sex as an expression of love, yet unless that has specifically been expressed, it's nowhere near a guarantee that such feelings exist. Be very careful not to fall into the trap of misinterpreting sex or using it to convince yourself that more may be going on than there actually is.

Then there are those people who engage in sex without even knowing their partner's last name or occupation—there's no relationship going on here, and although it may seem exciting, no romance either. In this case, one partner is using and the other partner is being used. There may be gratification in this, but there's no dignity. Without the energy of dignity, what really matters—the *long-term gratification of the happy life*—is impossible.

No matter what anyone says, *sex is never, ever casual; only the relationship is.* So if you think you're having casual sex, you need to know that what you're really doing is giving a very intimate part of yourself to a casual acquaintance. Does that honor you?

Keep in mind that if your choice to have sex comes from a dishonoring intention, it will only backfire. It sets you up as a heart apart. Eventually, whatever false source of happiness you're seeking will be defeated by the genuine unhappiness of a meaningless connection. Only a pure intention that comes from loving and honoring yourself and your partner can form the bonds of a truly harmonious relationship.

Sex and the Law of Harmony

The harmony between two people is based in a sense of equality. One person isn't in control, nor does one person have more power than the other—they see each other as equals, with equal needs and equally valid opinions and emotions.

You can't separate the quality of your sex life from what's going on elsewhere in the relationship. If you don't find respect, reciprocity, and real communication in your daily life, you certainly won't find these qualities in bed! If there's excessive arguing, nagging, or even indifference, the sex is bound to suffer. You may be able to compartmentalize the various aspects of your relationship, but your partner may not. Anger and criticism definitely decrease desire.

The quality and tone of a couple's communication means everything to the sharing of sexual pleasure. In a relationship where the communication is harsh, the sex can be frightening or oppressive. In a relationship where there's no communication at all, the sex is hollow and even disheartening—for at least one of the partners, if not both.

One example of this is a case that actually defies the usual stereotypes. Tom was a client of mine before he married Chloe. He was dealing with self-esteem issues, anxiety, and depression. In the depth of his difficulties, he met Chloe. At first, she seemed to be the answer to Tom's prayers. She listened to the problems that he needed to talk about and was affectionate and supportive—at least at the beginning.

Tom married Chloe long before they got a chance to really know each other. He'd been desperate to have a helpful partner during his difficult time. They got along fine at the onset, but it wasn't long before Tom began to notice that

Chloe was not as willing to listen as before. Nor was she as open with her feelings as he was.

Tom continued to work on his depression and anxiety, and eventually he made quite a bit of progress there. As he got better, though, Chloe became even more distant. Tom saw that there were huge differences in the ways that he and Chloe approached life. Once he was able to stop focusing on his own problems, it became uncomfortably clear that he and his wife had nearly opposite approaches to pretty much everything, including work, family, and money.

They'd had so many arguments that it became their main form of communication. Eventually they each shut down, moving from silence to hostility and back to silence again. In spite of all this, Chloe still desired a sexual relationship. One night, after an earlier hostile confrontation, she came home and initiated a romantic interlude. Tom hoped that this was a sign that she wanted to work things out. But when they got up the next day, things were precisely the same uncomfortable, uncommunicative way they'd been the day before.

Tom was devastated. Chloe had been able to compartmentalize where he could not. Perhaps Chloe was just more able to separate the sex from their problems, or perhaps she was hopeful that the sex itself would resolve things without having to work on the real issues. Either way, in Tom's heart the experience only drove more of a wedge between them, and to him, the experience was just more evidence that their problems were insurmountable. He could see no way out but divorce.

It takes much more than good sex to fix a relationship. In fact, it takes a good relationship to maintain a good sex life. Two people need a much closer connection—a communion of spirit—in order to sustain both the love and the sex of a lifelong relationship.

The Spiritual Connection

The word *passion* comes from the Latin word meaning "endure." Over time, it has come to describe any experience of great emotion, from joyous rapture to unimaginable suffering. The word "compassion" connects that same root word with the Latin prefix *com,* which means "together." *Compassion* signifies a sharing, sympathy, and understanding of deep emotional context.

Compassion is the heart of a healthy love relationship. There's nothing that brings the spirit of two people together like the genuinely shared experience of intimate love. This connection of spirit allows a couple to "endure together" and support each other through hardship and joy. Passion is the experience of mind and body, while compassion is the desire to connect heart-to-heart.

> *A spiritual relationship is the radiant result of mutually expressed compassion. The connection happens on all levels—emotional, intellectual, sensual, and sexual. It's a powerful resonance that emanates from one soul's recognition of another.*
>
> *This is the best kind of relationship, and it engenders the absolute best kind of sex. When you have this kind of union, intercourse becomes much more than physical pleasure. It's alive with waves of appreciation and bone-tingling love. When the joy is centered in the heart—not just in the genitals—there's nothing else like it!*

What does it take to create such a depth of feeling? To find the answer, we need to look once again to the *three R's* of *respect, reciprocity,* and *real communication.* These are the things that have the greatest impact on your sexual experience.

It's very difficult to be sexually attracted to someone you don't respect, and it's almost impossible to want to have sex with someone who you *know* doesn't respect you. As a result, the intention to maintain the high regard that you originally had for each other is very important in keeping the sexual interest high. To make sure this happens, you must do two things. You *must* let go of judgment, and you must focus on the value that each person brings to the relationship. In other words, you have to consciously look for and remember all that there is to appreciate in each other.

An intrinsic part of developing a deep spiritual connection is choosing to see the heart of the person instead of their habits. So many times in a relationship, people focus on the annoying little idiosyncrasies of their partner. They lose sight of the bigger picture and base their partner's value on those negative qualities alone.

Take, for instance, a former client of mine. Debby had been dissatisfied with her marriage for quite some time. She and her husband, Sam, got along well when it came to dealing with the daily matters of life, but they hadn't felt close in a long time. They'd been married for about 12 years when I first started seeing Debby, and they'd fallen into a typical pattern of quiet indifference.

Basically, they each led their own lives. They liked different sports, were busy in their own careers, and were very active in social and political functions. They became what's called "married singles," two people who lead virtually single lives within the parameters of a married relationship. Over the years, they'd arrived at an unspoken agreement to remain distant but civil. They communicated with each other concerning the logistical things that came up—but not much more. Naturally, their sex life went down the tubes.

Debby realized that she no longer respected Sam the way she used to. She knew that he was good at his job, but she tended to perceive him as shallow everywhere else. Little things began to annoy her about him, like how he ate and what he liked to watch on television. She started focusing all of her attention on his irritating idiosyncrasies, and of course, she found even more. Debby began judging his character solely on that focus, and in time, she totally lost sight of all of the wonderful characteristics that had initially drawn her to Sam. Her life felt empty—with the loss of communication came the loss of respect, and the emotional reciprocity wasn't far behind. She and Sam had become virtual strangers, each alone in a life together.

Then something happened that changed everything: Sam got sick. He had to quit work, and Debby had to adjust her schedule in order to take him to all of his doctor's appointments. So of course, they started spending much more time together. Perhaps it was that, or maybe it was facing a serious illness together, but they began to be more open with each other. They started to talk about their feelings and how things had changed in their relationship. They discussed what they missed about each other and why they'd stopped talking.

Debby soon realized that she had shortchanged Sam. Through their rekindled communication, she found a renewed respect for him. She now knew that he hadn't become shallow; they'd *both become superficial in how they related to each other.*

Debby and Sam actually became excited about getting to know each other again. They spent much more time together, and they discussed everything—there was a lot to catch up on, and they enjoyed the catching up. They even started having sex again. Fortunately, Sam recovered—not only did he get his health back, but they got their marriage back. What seemed to be a potentially terrible problem actually turned out to be a gift.

You don't have to wait for your partner to get sick to let go of the judgment. You don't have to wait for a catastrophe to renew your communication. Don't make the same mistake Debby and Sam made—they lived in the same house, but not in the same relationship. Their relationship had been sacrificed on the altar of self-absorption.

If you want to maintain a healthy, happy relationship for life, you need to continually renew your interest in each other. Take the steps to get closer. Don't get sidetracked by life, becoming more distant over time. The more time you spend together—the more you communicate instead of judge—the more you'll revel in each other's love. This is sure to keep the sexual interest exciting and alive.

Forever Foreplay

Familiarity may not breed contempt, but it often fosters disinterest. As life becomes more and more predictable, you need to stay focused on each other to keep the sexual interest high.

Your sex life isn't limited to a series of sexual encounters. All of your shared experiences factor into your sexual relationship. Whether or not you feel encouraged, safe, intellectually stimulated, or emotionally embraced, all of this is part of the ongoing foreplay that arouses the sexual interest between you. Feeling accepted and knowing that you're understood definitely creates a sexual connection. This rules out criticism, jealousy, and chronic anger. A wounded heart closes itself to love. With each new wound, the heart needs to shut down even more. The end result is a heart that can't see love and has no desire to make it.

It's important that each person realizes that the emotional relationship sets the stage for sexual interest and arousal. It's far too simplistic to think that sex can be good—or even should be expected—no matter what the rest of the relationship is like. You can't expect your sex life to be hot if you treat each other coldly.

You need to love and support each other, both in and out of the bedroom. There should be a mutual intention to create reciprocity—in life and in your sexual connection.

While sex isn't likely to be the same experience for both of you 100 percent of the time, it should be equally satisfying most of the time. With both respect and reciprocity, the physical relationship can be a vibrant and exciting one.

Finally, real communication is a must in creating a physically loving connection. We communicate in many ways—through touch, looks, and our words. With the right approach to your care of each other, your whole life can stimulate a deeper sexual connection.

A touch and a smile in the morning, an encouraging word in the afternoon—this is the foreplay of an evening's sexual interlude. Loving treatment is what most encourages a desiring heart, and making love with your words is the best foreplay ever. Give words of praise and whispers of admiration. Steal a kiss; caress a cheek. Show that you care.

> *Being in a loving relationship means making love in all sorts of ways every day. It doesn't have to be sexual—it could be sensual, tactile, or verbal. Any little thing can be an act of making love—from holding hands, to making a meal, to saying thank you. If such things were seen in this context, instead of as obligations, the entire nature of your relationship would change. Bring a loving intention to all that you do for—and with—each other. Every time you do, you will be making love.*

Tenderness of touch and word excites the body as well the soul. Always express your respect and your affection. This is the real source of sexual pleasure. When each person brings a loved and loving heart to bed, the sex—and the relationship—need never end.

❧ CHAPTER FIFTEEN ❧

Saying Good-bye

"Learn to stand alone,
secure in your own virtues and self-worth."
— Paramahansa Yogananda

Nothing is quite as devastating as the loss of a love. Whether through a breakup, divorce, or death, losing someone you truly love can be one of the most stressful and traumatic experiences of your life. Even if you're the one making the choice to move on, the decision to do so can be fraught with difficulty and discomfort.

By being aware of the Universal Laws *before* you get into a relationship, you can save yourself a lot of pain and problems later on. Attracting a relationship isn't the same as making a relationship last. Attracting the *right* relationship must be the priority if you hope to never have to say good-bye.

Everyone reacts to loss differently. Some people obsess about their loss and seem to live in endless mourning. Others go into denial and act like it never happened, thinking that if they ignore it, the pain will go away. Many people get angry and never let their anger go; they take it out on themselves and the people around them. Then, when they finally do get into another relationship, they try to make their new partner pay for what happened to them in the past. Some people throw themselves into work or social activities in order to get distracted. Others find their distraction through addictions such as food, alcohol, drugs, and even sex. Still others isolate themselves, shutting themselves off from other emotional connections, hoping to prevent any future pain.

Obviously, none of these extremes is an ideal approach to handling the loss of a love. They may work for a little while, but they certainly don't provide healthy ways to move on. Nor do they create the kind of energy that will help you attract the successful, lifelong relationship you were looking for in the first place.

There are steps you can take to help you move on and even magnetize something far better—these are **the separation skills.** Let yourself work on them little by little. Letting go of a relationship takes time, but if you follow each of the following steps, you'll be able to create a new energy . . . and a new life.

Separation Skill #1: Allow Yourself to Grieve

Grief is one of the hardest things to deal with in life. People intellectually acknowledge their loss, but they often don't know what to do with their feelings about it. They may be beside themselves with emotion, yet are unable to identify or express what they're going through.

The loss of a love can be all-consuming. For a while, it imposes its dark presence on you every day. You wake up in the morning and reach for your loved one, but no one is there. You pick up the phone, but there's no one to call. You go shopping and automatically reach for their favorite items. With every one of these experiences—and hundreds more—you feel the loss anew.

Grief is very real and very painful. It can't be denied, although many people try. It can't be minimized or dismissed, although many people force themselves to shake off their tears after a very brief time. Not allowing yourself to grieve is a huge mistake, for carrying unexpressed grief with you creates a heaviness to your energy that's often palpable. You may be in denial, going through your regular routine and acting like nothing ever happened, but your energy is screaming your misery. You're broadcasting a depressing frequency. More than that, you're weaving into your life a new set of toxic and traumatized beliefs that will affect all that you do.

If you don't allow yourself to feel the emotions *of an experience, you'll carry the* conclusions *from that experience with you. Once in place, these conclusions work their way into your beliefs, thoughts, behaviors, and consciousness, generating a darkening resonant frequency.*

This is very important. Do you really want your frequency to be sending out waves of unexpressed pain and loss? What do you think you will attract in return?

Trauma-based beliefs are emotionally charged. One common toxic conclusion that springs out of the grief of a broken relationship is "Love is unsafe." If you don't allow yourself to *experience* your grief and *release* it, new thoughts of potential love will be threatening to you. Your negativity will insulate you in an energetic black cloud, protecting you from being hurt in this way again.

Only by feeling *will you be able to release, and only by releasing will you be able to be free. Grief isn't the tragedy, it's the cleansing process that deals with the tragedy. In time, it helps you turn your pain into knowledge and even power.*

Your emotional makeup is like a garden—there are wonderful flowers and difficult weeds. You have to get down in the dirt and pull up the weeds, although it may mean getting messy. Even if those weeds are prickly and painful, you have to deal with them or they'll take over your emotional life. All you'll have left is a tangled, ugly mess where no beauty can grow.

Grief is one of those weeds, a big one. If you think you can end a relationship and never deal with the pain, don't be surprised if not much good grows in your life afterward. In fact, your intention to deny your pain and pretend nothing happened could actually backfire and turn your grief into an obsession.

I had a client named Diane who left a verbally abusive relationship after four years. After nearly two years of dating other people with nothing turning out well, she came to talk to me about her relationship experience. When I asked her if she allowed herself to grieve over the loss of that four-year relationship, she made it clear that she hadn't.

"What was there to be sad about?" she said. "He was so awful, I should have been glad to be away from it."

In spite of this cavalier sentiment, Diane found herself thinking about him much of the time, even though it had already been two years since their breakup. She still felt angry and hurt—angry about the way he treated her, yet hurt that he never tried to get back together with her after she'd left him. She often wondered what he was doing now and if he had found someone new. Although she stuffed her emotions down and said she wasn't sad, she couldn't stop her thoughts from going back and reviewing the whole experience over and over. She'd become obsessed.

What she hadn't done—but needed very much to do—was to allow herself to truly feel her feelings, both her anger and her grief. She had to acknowledge that she truly did experience a loss. She lost a relationship in which she'd placed her hopes. Of course, this wasn't the relationship that she really wanted, but it did represent something positive to her. He may have been a cad, but he also had other qualities that she liked, or else why would she have gotten involved with him in the first place? And why stay with him for four years?

When Diane started to let her feelings out, she was amazed at the amount of grief that came up. She wrote in her journal. She talked about the way he had made her feel. She acknowledged what she missed about him, in spite of the fact that he wasn't always kind. She dug into her feelings and got them out. The more she did so, the less she found herself thinking about him. In time, she had no feelings at all about the relationship except genuine relief that it was truly in the past. She'd cleared out all that old, contaminated energy. She was free of the obsession and happier than she'd been in six years.

Stay with the Pain and See It Through

No matter how tempted you are to run away from it, don't deny or minimize your grief. Grief, like anger and other emotional weeds, only gets bigger if left unattended. In time, you may find that you have twice as much work getting out the grief than you would have had if you'd dealt with it right away. And you'll be forced to do even more work realigning your thinking after the new, traumatized thoughts have taken hold.

Don't be afraid of your pain. Instead of running away from it, let yourself sit with it and breathe into it. You're performing a sort of emotional surgery on yourself, and the only way to get rid of the pain is to go inside it, see it, feel it, and then bring it out. Talk, cry, or write it out. Move it out. Don't hurry through your grief—it will take you however long it takes you. You're the one who has to live with the energies that you carry—don't let others rush you into denial.

Having said that, it's also *very important* not to turn your grief into obsession. Some people actually redefine themselves by their loss. The emptiness is so all-consuming that it eventually takes on a life of its own. This is especially true if they'd previously been defining themselves by their relationship.

Allow yourself to grieve when you feel the emotions come up, and permit yourself to let go when you feel the timing is right. With enough expression, you should start to feel yourself letting go more and more. After a while, you will begin to see some balance in your reactions.

Separation Skill #2: Express Your Anger Appropriately

Closely tied to the energy of grief is the energy of anger. In fact, having anger is a natural part of the grief process. You can't be in a relationship without ever experiencing something to get angry about. You can't leave a relationship (or be left by someone) without having anger either.

Living with unexpressed anger bears the same results as living with unexpressed grief. It builds up inside of you and changes who you are. It alters your emotions, thoughts, and perceptions, resulting in a dramatic reversal of your personal energy.

> *Any loss, no matter what the circumstances, automatically elicits at least some anger. Denying it or rationalizing it into submission doesn't make it disappear. Only feeling it, acknowledging it, and letting it out will make it go away. Whether it's grief or rage, you simply can't move on without getting the real feelings out.*

When you don't know exactly what you're feeling or why, do some emotional mining. Sift through your thoughts and experiences, and keep on digging. You may have to go through a lot of dirt before you strike gold and finally uncover what the source of your deeper issue really is.

Getting It Out

In order to get into your deepest feelings, use a notebook dedicated solely to your relationship responses. Write your feelings in the form of a letter to your love. Since you never have to send it, you're free to say anything and everything that comes up. Add to this letter anytime an emotion arises, and say whatever you need to say—without editing yourself.

To help get at your genuine reactions, here's a list of *starter sentences* to complete. These phrases are the beginnings of thoughts that will help you uncover your emotional truths. They can help you express those things that you may not even be aware of.

- *Dear . . .*
- *I feel . . .*
- *What I need to tell you is . . .*
- *It really hurt me when . . .*
- *It really made me angry when . . .*
- *It's so hard for me to understand . . .*
- *How could you . . .*
- *Why didn't you . . .*
- *Do you know how it felt when . . .*
- *What I never told you was . . .*
- *If you'd only . . .*
- *If I'd only . . .*
- *If we'd only . . .*
- *I remember when . . .*
- *When I think of how . . .*
- *What I miss the most is . . .*
- *I was so hoping that . . .*
- *I'm still feeling the pain from . . .*
- *What you'll never know is . . .*
- *I loved you because . . .*
- *I need to let you go because . . .*

Use these starters to help open the door to your feelings. Write letters to anyone who may have hurt you, whether they be lovers, family, or friends. Get it out and let it go. You need to deal with old grief and anger so you can truly and freely move on. You never know what fears, addictions, or other problems may be coming from old anger or pain being held in.

Remember, as long as you're carrying the emotions, you're also holding the negative beliefs those emotions have generated. And the more highly charged the emotion, the more strongly held the belief. You absolutely must turn that cognitive energy around! Take note of your unhealthy conclusions—about relationships or anything else—and then *change them.* You'll be surprised at the cleansing that takes place.

One word of caution about anger related to a previous relationship: Expressing your anger doesn't mean getting revenge. Trying to get revenge only compromises your honor at a time when your self-esteem is already feeling vulnerable. Revenge may feel good at the time, but it's bound to backfire on you energetically. It ultimately costs you your dignity—not only in others' eyes, but more important, in your own. This is far too high a price to pay for a few moments of meaningless vindication. If you express your anger appropriately and choose to only engage in honoring behavior, you'll eventually get your satisfaction by magnetizing the magnificent life you deserve.

Separation Skill #3:
Be Realistic: Do *Not* Fantasize Your Loss

This is a common reaction for people who are in the process of breaking up. In their selective memory, they lose sight of the reality, *the complete reality,* of their relationship. They fantasize about *what could have been* without recalling what really was. Even people who have been seriously mistreated often focus on their good memories, minimizing the bad. This is especially true for those people who turn to love in order to compensate for what they feel is missing in themselves. They start out genuinely grieving what they lost—missing the fun, camaraderie, and excitement.

But then their pain goes deeper, for without the distraction of the relationship, they're forced to become reacquainted with their own emptiness. They obsess about the good memories because for those few shining moments, they were lulled into thinking that their emptiness had been filled up. But they were never *really* filled up, just as the fantasy was never *really* the relationship.

Don't exaggerate the power that a relationship has brought to your life. To live with the fantasy that you ever were or ever could be filled up by another person perpetuates a lie. It never happened! Believing it only dishonors and disempowers you and sets you up for unavoidable failure in the future—pursuing an end that can never be achieved, dismissing yourself and your happiness in the process.

Fantasizing the loss prolongs the grief process and exaggerates feelings of hopelessness. It causes you to long for the lost relationship no matter what the reality of that relationship might have been. You only end up putting your life—and your responsibility for creating your own happiness—on hold.

This happened to one of my clients recently when her boyfriend broke up with her. Interestingly, Sharon had been unsure about staying in the relationship to begin with, as Joel was distant and often very critical. He was also only minimally available to her. And yet, on his better days, he was capable of being downright charming, so much so that Sharon ultimately chose to ignore his little criticisms. Sharon was very intelligent, and in Joel, she found a mind that could not only keep up with hers but also challenge it. They both had an acerbic sense of humor, and they laughed a lot. They had long talks about politics, philosophy, art, and literature.

Unfortunately, when Joel broke up with Sharon, these better attributes were all that she could focus on. Remembering how smart and funny he was, she forgot all of the times that he'd been unavailable to her. All of the times he made her feel small and insignificant with some cutting remark seemed to slip her mind. Putting all that aside, she now felt she'd lost her best friend, someone who made her laugh and think. Over and over again, she relived their tender moments, remembering Joel's finer qualities. She didn't think she'd ever find anyone as "good" as him again.

Sharon's perception was distorted. She felt much more grief than anger, and was totally absorbed in her loss. She hadn't realized it, but she was fantasizing her loss and idealizing her partner. She got trapped in this downward spiral, becoming obsessed with what she thought was missing—yet all along what had been missing was real love and respect.

Sharon was spinning her wheels. She was beginning to find it difficult to work, and she was constantly tempted to call Joel under some fabricated pretext or another. She knew she had to do something to break this cycle, so she wrote letters to Joel and completed the starter sentences listed above to get in touch with her anger. She also had to do a lot of reality testing where the relationship was concerned. For a while, she had to be very strict with her cognitive interventions. Every time she'd think longingly of something they'd shared, she would consider the relationship in its entirety. She forced herself to recall the many times Joel had been unavailable or critical. She soon realized that there had been many more of those hurtful episodes than the tender moments she'd been obsessing about.

Sharon freed herself from the illusion of paradise lost. Her next guy wasn't someone just as "good"—he was far better.

Her decision to see the relationship for what it was brought her a happier one. She now wonders what she ever saw in the man she thought she "couldn't live without."

The Gift in the Grief

When you're looking back on your relationship, you have to see the *whole* picture, the good with the bad. You need to remember the loss as a whole, not just the individual episodes where things seemed perfect. If you catch yourself daydreaming about those wonderful moments, stop and consider the *entire* experience. In your journal, remember to write about the whole relationship. Allow yourself to grieve the good as well as acknowledge the bad.

Being realistic doesn't mean becoming cynical or jaded. If you're leaving a relationship or have been left by someone, then there are lessons to learn. It's now time to look for the gift in the grief. If you fantasize the loss, you'll be blind to the real mechanics of your relationship patterns. You won't be able to think clearly about what went on and what you could have done differently to be more self-honoring.

As painful as it may seem, there's a valuable lesson in this experience. Whether it's self-prioritizing, or a renewed determination to be more discerning in your relationship choices, you have the power to turn this pain into a plus. You can learn from this experience, but you'll never do so if you keep deluding yourself about it.

Fantasizing your loss carries with it three very significant energetic problems:

1. **Falsely fantasizing about what could have been shifts your focus. It forces you to always focus on what you lack, instead of what you have.** While you must allow yourself to genuinely grieve what you've lost, you must

also constantly acknowledge all that you have, relationship or not. This will be absolutely necessary if you don't want to attract a similar situation of loss in the future. Remember, *that which you focus on expands.*

2. **If you're idealizing the loss, you're also idealizing the person. In idealizing your partner, you may be making yourself "wrong" or faulty in some way.** People are on different paths and different places on those paths. If your two paths don't match, it doesn't have to mean there's anything wrong with you. Don't torment yourself with the "something's wrong with me" assumption, or the next person you magnetize will assume the same.

3. **Idealizing the relationship only keeps your two energies attached.** Even if you never see the person again, the fantasy keeps you longing, and the longing keeps you connected. Ruminating about what could have been only makes you hold on to it more—even if there's nothing to hold on to. This is a problem because the ultimate healing of any relationship loss is finally letting it go.

Separation Skill #4: When It's Over, Let It Go!

One of the hardest things about ending a relationship is having the courage to *really* let it go. In some ways, we can become dependent on a relationship by virtue of its habitual nature alone. But holding on to a lifeless relationship isn't only unhealthy, it's disastrous to your frequency.

Staying emotionally attached when your partner has

moved on is energetic suicide. It keeps your personal energy tied up in knots, and everything else in your life gets wrapped up in this tangled mess. Your frequency isn't open, and people who might otherwise tune in to you pick up only noise instead. Your longing becomes a black hole of desire—you're funneling your hope and intention into a deep and empty well that will, in time, suck you in, too. It's so clearly destructive to your resonance and emotional well-being that nothing good can come from it.

Not letting go breaks *all* of the Universal Laws, and it will stop you cold if you have any intention to have a new, mutually loving relationship. First, it dishonors you and destroys your dignity. You simply can't align yourself with the Law of Magnetism if you're pining after someone who no longer feels the same way.

Second, it muddies up your pure desire. If you're still longing for someone who doesn't reciprocate, then your intention is way out of balance. You're not motivated by a desire to have a *mutual* relationship; you're spurred on by more desperate needs, like the fear of being rejected or the need to control the other person's perception of you. This resonates with urgency and stimulates the Law of Paradoxical Intent. In your desperation to hold on, you assume that this is the only relationship for you and that it's impossible to find another. This totally corrupts your magnetic energy, and the fear behind the urgency becomes a self-fulfilling prophecy. Such desperation can only result in pushing the relationship away further, along with any other that may come your way.

Finally, this unrequited love throws you out of harmony. Harmony is balance. Your need to cling to a dead relationship obviously puts you out of balance with your partner's energy, but more important, it puts you out of balance with yourself. Your energy is poured into a place where it can't be returned, leaving you feeling isolated and alone.

This emotional isolation then moves you out of harmony

with the Universe. You'll always find yourself out of sync because your focus isn't on your life but on something that refuses to be a part of your life. You become a broken cog in the clockwork of Universal harmony; nothing wonderful can connect with you, and you keep spinning in useless motion. *The negative consequences of staying emotionally attached to someone who has moved on cannot be overemphasized.* Your energies are already entangled with this person. Even if you could disengage the moment the relationship is over, it would take some time and pure intention to clear your personal energy field of the old resonance.

> *By staying emotionally attached, especially if you still feel longing, need, or urgency, you're actually broadcasting a message of unavailability to the world. Your obsessed frequency is saying that you're already in a relationship. Even if that relationship is only in your imagination, you're putting up an energetic wall to prevent any future loves from entering the picture.*

But when you finally let go of the emotional connection—when you release any residual feelings, especially feelings of hope or longing to get back together—you open up a clearly resonant space in your willingness to receive. Your message to the Universe is now: *"I'm unattached. I'm free. Send my ideal partner to me."* All of the old, self-imposed barriers will start to come down when you make this choice.

When it's over, let it go. Face the unknown and make it your own. Don't blame your partner or beat yourself up. Don't make yourself wrong, unworthy, or faulty. Stop reviewing and reliving every last detail of your relationship trying to figure out what happened. Let it go and keep on letting it go. The following guidelines should help.

Guidelines for Really Letting Go of the Relationship

1. As hard as it may seem, **don't take the loss personally.** When you do so, you make it seem as if there's something wrong with you. This can only shift your self-perception to one of victim or loser. Neither is your truth! This kind of personalization won't help you recover from your grief. And the catastrophic thinking it creates will really muck up your energetic projection!

2. **Maintain your dignity.** Don't beg, lie, or manipulate in order to try to make the pain stop. Don't go in pursuit of your ex—don't follow, stalk, or harass. It's beneath you and dishonors you.

3. **Stop the obsessive thinking.** Always, always, always intervene on pointless ruminations, such as: "I wonder what he's doing," or "I wonder if she is seeing someone new," or "Why can't it be like it was before?" This gets you nowhere but deeper in your grief.

4. **Don't catastrophize.** You *will* get through this. You *will* move on. You will even find love again—if that's what you want.

5. **Practice all of the separation skills.** Letting go takes time; and practice makes progress. It's your intention to move on that counts. Create that intention, and then muster up the courage to make it real.

You're not doing yourself any favors by holding on. It doesn't promote feelings of optimism or encourage thoughts of self-love. And it's an absolute poison to your personal energy field!

> *The Universe loves to fill a void. If you can take the risk of really letting go, you'll be cutting the energetic bonds that keep you tied up. It may take some courage to move into that open (and seemingly empty) space where you alone are responsible. But when you do, the Universe will respond by flooding that space with love.*

If you don't let go, however, there will be no void to fill. You yourself will be cluttering up that space with your own obsession and need for control. With that as your resonant core, how can you attract the loving energy that your heart is aching for?

Separation Skill #5: Master the Art of Being Alone

The Law of Paradoxical Intent dictates that the sooner you can be at peace with being alone, the sooner you'll project the kind of energy that magnetizes more peace and happiness—and more love—into your life. The paradox comes when you use your fear of being alone as your motivation for pursuing relationships. *If you feel you can't be happy while alone, it practically ensures that you will stay both unhappy and alone.*

Being comfortable with being alone speaks to your security and self-definition, as well as your capacity for happiness. You must evaluate your perception of being alone to see how it impacts your intention. If you perceive being alone as a burden—a miserable condition that must be avoided at all costs—then your intention to find a partner will be driven by urgency and project a very desperate energy. If, on the other hand, you perceive being alone as a wonderful adventure and a great opportunity to address your own needs and create your own happiness, your intention to have a relationship will be based in trust and project a vibrantly magnetic energy.

You don't have to equate being alone with being lonely. *If you feel that your life is empty, it's up to you to fill it.* A full life is one with a *personal purpose*—one that's separate from the relationship you're in, or the one you're looking for. You *can* create a fulfilling life for yourself—and you don't need a partner to make it so.

> *To create a thriving and happy single life, you must first be comfortable with your own company. You need to see your time spent alone as time spent in good society. Look forward to your time together with yourself. If you don't enjoy your own company, nobody else will.*
>
> *Your time alone is one of your greatest resources. Use it creatively. Enjoy it. Make plans* with *yourself* for *yourself. Implement a new lifestyle of rejuvenation and self-care.*

Mastering the art of being alone means that you are truly disengaging and cleansing your energies of the old attachment, creating an open and healthy space for the Universe to fill. The best way to magnetize love from any corridor is to master your relationship with yourself, to arrive at a place of genuine autonomy and self-reliance.

It's the definitive act of trust to say, "If I have to spend the rest of my life alone, that's okay. I'm going to make it the happiest, most rewarding life ever." This is the ultimate surrender to the Universe, and it brings wonderful (and sometimes immediate) results—when it honestly comes from the heart.

Separation Skill #6: Choose to *Create* a Life of Happiness

There are two basic ways in which people approach happiness. Some people *pursue* happiness; others *create* it. Those that *pursue* happiness are chasing after it. Their fundamental view of happiness is an external one. Their assumption is that happiness comes mainly through other people or through the achievement of external goals, such as financial gain, career success, or material acquisitions.

Those who *create* happiness perceive it more as a state of mind, something intrinsic to the process of life, regardless of externals. Rather than waiting and hoping that their happiness will come later, these people make choices in their thoughts and behaviors that focus on happiness now. They have an awareness of options, a proactive mentality that says, "Today I'll create happiness at every opportunity. I'll be playful and optimistic and look for the joy in even the smallest tasks."

When you find that your relationship is ending, what is your intention? Do you intend to *create* happiness, or do you intend to *pursue* it? If your intention is to create it, you should be able to move on much more easily. If, however, you're a pursuer of happiness, you'll have a very difficult time dealing with the grief. You'll be constantly obsessing on the happiness you've lost, filling your energy with past-remembering and future-yearning, rather than present-peacefulness.

If you want to create your own happiness, the first thing you must do is to stop creating your own misery. This requires an *aggressive* plan to intervene on *all* self-sabotaging and self-dishonoring choices. Stop the perfectionism, the catastrophizing, the brooding, and self-recriminations. Stop it all now!

Whether we want to believe it or not, we ourselves are the biggest source of our own unhappiness. By choosing loving thoughts, healthy behaviors, and positive things to focus on, we can stop being the cause of our own troubles. When we adopt a playful attitude—a determination to lighten up—we can learn to enjoy life and create a truly happy and brilliantly magnetic energy.

Oh, Do Joy!

If you've been a happiness chaser throughout your life, you need to become a happiness creator. You need to provide for yourself that which you're looking for from others. Ask yourself what it is that makes you happy, and then *take responsibility for creating that in your life.* If it's encouragement, give encouragement to yourself. If you need more fun, find ways to bring more fun into your life. *Ultimately you need to establish two things: a joy-seeking attitude and an appreciation consciousness.*

An attitude that seeks joy is one that approaches the tasks of life with an intention to make them more enjoyable. An appreciation consciousness carries an ever-present awareness of what one has to be grateful for instead of an ongoing concern of what one lacks. Whatever we're most conscious of expands. To be chronically conscious of your loss only expands your experience of lack and attracts even more loss. To be conscious of what you have to appreciate—in spite of your recent loss—will cause your experience of appreciation to expand. It will magnetize more and more things to be grateful for, and you'll find your life overflowing with wonderful people and enjoyable experiences.

For more than 20 years, I've encouraged my clients to keep an "Appreciation and Acknowledgment Notebook." This is what I suggest: At the end of each day, write three things that you've appreciated during the day, such as a beautiful sunset, a conversation with a friend, some quiet time alone, or even a good movie. *In addition,* write down at least two times a day when you acknowledge or appreciate something about yourself, such as a decision you made, a moment of courage, a choice to be self-honoring, or a change you made in your energy.

If we only look outside of ourselves for the things that we appreciate, we're just going halfway. It's important to see value in every external thing, but it's also important to acknowledge the value and power *within ourselves*. Even if we're at a place in our lives when we can find almost nothing outside of ourselves to appreciate, we can always appreciate our own strength, dignity, courage, and fortitude.

The Appreciation and Acknowledgment Notebook is a very important daily process for two reasons. First, it causes you to develop a greater awareness of the enjoyable and valuable experiences of your daily life. You no longer have to wait for special occasions to see the pleasure of things. And second, it helps you acknowledge yourself more and brings you a greater awareness of the options you have to make better choices—choices that you know you'll appreciate later. In time, you'll actually look for opportunities to display more courage and take more responsibility for yourself and your happiness.

Happiness is the emotion of appreciation. If you think about the times that you've been truly happy, you were—on some level—in the state of appreciation. Whether you're conscious of it or not, every time you're happy, you are celebrating something you appreciate.

In this way, appreciation expands your happiness consciousness. It's a dynamic part of living in harmony with yourself and with the world. When you appreciate, you take your power back. Your happiness and enjoyment are no longer random experiences based on the circumstances of your life. They are choices you make, emotional interpretations you actively create.

Affirmations for Creating Happiness

- *I deserve to be happy. I'm creating my happiness now.*

- *Every day, I'm increasing my focus of appreciation and self-acknowledgment.*

- *I'm learning to love myself and my life.*

- *I'm learning to appreciate myself and my life.*

- *I have the power to create happiness every day.*

- *I look for joy and take action to create it every day.*

- *I'm finding little things to enjoy in all the daily tasks of life.*

- *I'm developing a more playful and fun-loving attitude about everything.*

- *I choose to embrace all of the happiness that life has to offer.*

- *Every day is a new opportunity for joy!*

Successfully Separated—So What's Next?

The process of engaging in the separation skills takes some time. Only you can determine how much time you need to really feel finished and free. Take as much time as you need, but be sure you keep *doing the process* till you're done. When you feel ready to move on, write another letter to your lost love. By now you should have written at least a few letters in your journal, expressing your feelings of anger, grief, and loss. Yet it will still be important to write another, a good-bye letter.

Whatever feelings you may have left, get them out.

When you're done with that, let your lover go. Say good-bye. Bless them and release them, but write your intention to be finished with them. Say whatever you need to say to make that happen. When you're done, write all your good-byes, and let them go.

Finish the process in a ceremony. Burn that letter. Cut it up and affirm that you're cutting your energetic connection, or throw it away and affirm you're throwing away the pain. When you've completed this process, give yourself some time. Every time you see the places and things that remind you of that person, affirm your good-byes once again. Say out loud, if you can, "I release you from this place. I let you go." Take a deep breath and affirm, "I'm free."

Once you've written your last good-bye, you still have one more letter to write, not to your love, but to the Universe. This is a "hello" letter. It's time to welcome in your new life, and if you desire it, your new love. List all of the things you're looking forward to experiencing in the time ahead of you. Also list the qualities you'd like to find in your new partner when another relationship comes your way.

Some people find the idea of programming a relationship to be too calculating. But this is one of the most important events of your life. You consider the particulars when planning a career, picking a college, or even buying a car. Why shouldn't you consider what you want in a relationship? There's no longer any need to leave your relationship destiny up to chance. You understand the dynamics of the Universal Laws—if you place your order and create the same energy, the Universe *will* make the delivery.

Make a list of all of the characteristics you find important in a partner. If intellect or sensitivity are qualities you admire, include them. What about maturity and financial responsibility? If you want someone who's artistic, musical, or interested in sports, include that, too. A sense of humor is such a plus, I encourage everyone to consider it in their projection. Life is a lot easier when you're living with someone who's playful.

It's safe for you to be selective. Let go of the old, limited mentality, and know that there *is* someone out there for you, someone who demonstrates the qualities you admire. You don't have to settle anymore. Remember when you're doing your programming to include the absolute necessities of a healthy relationship: *respect, reciprocity,* and *real communication.* If these aren't qualities your partner is capable of, none of the other qualities will matter.

Also, be very careful to program what you want, *not what you don't want!* If you continue to focus on all that was wrong with your last partner, you'll only attract another variation of that experience. This is why releasing the emotions—as well as the attachment—is so important.

You must intervene on your fear of attracting the same old energy. Stop obsessing about your ex-partner's faults. Change your intention, and know that you can magnetize wonderful, new qualities. Let the past go, and be optimistic about your future. Once you've decided what you want in a partner, write it all down. Affirm that you, too, demonstrate the qualities that you desire in another. Notice in your daily life how you can fine-tune the same qualities within yourself. After all, if you want to attract it, you have to project it.

When you meditate—or when you go to bed—visualize your energetic self moving out into the Universe. See yourself as a shiny beacon of light, projecting the very energy you're looking for in brilliant waves in all directions. Affirm your intention to attract your ideal partner, one who possesses the qualities you desire. Then once you've sent your energy out, completely let it go! Release it with trust into the great field of all possibilities. Release it in time and space, and wait with patience and surrender.

Programming is the act of putting conscious thought and clear expectations into what you want. This will help you be more selective and more self-honoring when entering new relationship territory. If you're clear about what you want, you won't be so easily persuaded to accept what you don't want. With patience, clarity, and courage, your goal will be achieved.

Don't be frantic. The Universe responds to your energy of self-honoring and your intention to accept only healthy and loving treatment. As long as you're providing these parts of the equations, the only unknowns will be where and when. Trust that the best is yet to come, and it certainly will!

Losing a Relationship and Finding Love

I have a friend named Rosie. She's a smart, pretty, and vibrant woman with a smile that reaches right into your heart. Rosie works as an event planner in London, orchestrating meetings, conferences, and all sorts of grand parties.

I was at one of those soirées a few years ago—a beautiful dinner party overlooking the Thames—when Rosie started talking to me about her relationship. She'd been dating a man for a couple of years and had recently moved in with him. She referred to him as a "good" man. But they had very different natures, and they spent a lot of time apart. It soon became clear by the way Rosie talked that something very important was missing.

Since this dinner was such a big event, and all of the people that Rosie worked with had brought a date, I asked her to introduce him to me. I thought this might provide me with some clues about how they related to each other. But when Rosie told me he wasn't there—because she hadn't invited him—it gave me the biggest clue of all.

"How do I know that he's *the one?*" she'd asked earlier.

I told her that I thought his absence—as a result of *her* preference—gave her the answer to that question. If he wasn't there, he wasn't the one. After all, if she didn't want to spend this one spectacular and rather romantic night with him, how could she want to spend all the rest of the nights of her life with him?

Rosie and I talked at length about what was going on in the relationship. She realized that she'd been staying more out of habit than love. Staying seemed to make it easier, but it wasn't truthful. The superficial nature of their connection threw them out of harmony with each other, and as a result, their relationship had become empty. In spite of all that, leaving was still a scary proposition. Letting go of the familiar—especially something that seems so safe—in order to move into the unknown can be very frightening. The Universe may love to fill a void, but for it to do so, you first have to create that void.

> *To clear your energy, you need to uncouple and allow the emptiness to surround you. But taking this risk of truly letting go brings a dynamic change to your magnetic energy. It expands your resonance. It unscrambles your frequency, making it clearer and allowing others to connect more easily. On top of that, the choice to let go broadcasts signals of self-trust. It reverberates your willingness to take responsibility for your own happiness, the resonance of which is the finest signal you can send out into the world.*

When Rosie realized that she'd been staying for safety instead of real love, she mustered up the courage to say good-bye. She knew she deserved something better, something real. She did the programming visualization and worked on changing her energy. And she had very good news when I was back in London for another conference two years later—she'd completely let her old relationship go and had been dating someone new. This time it was entirely different. Rosie was even more vivacious than usual—it turned out that Stan, her new love, was exactly what she had been looking for.

I was fortunate to have dinner with them both and could see how very much they resonated with each other. It was obvious that they connected on a very deep level. Stan was vibrant, playful, and loving—a mirror to Rosie's own energy. This time, they came to the party together. There was no question about him being *the one*—the depth of their love was visible for all to see.

It's been over a year since then, and Rosie and Stan have gotten married. They've traveled extensively together and have many more exciting plans for the future. Rosie is now glad she left that safe, yet stultified, situation. If she hadn't, she would never have been free to meet her true love.

It may be difficult, even frightening, to say good-bye. But the courage to truly let go will open Universal doors for you. There are endless opportunities provided by the Law of Harmony. We are all linked in great fields of resonating energies—global connections that reverberate with like frequencies. Those connections not only result in romantic couplings, but in consequences that are more profound and farther reaching than we could ever fathom.

❧ EPILOGUE ❧

Love in the Universe

> *"All people are cells in
> the one divine organism, The Divine Body.
> That should be your faith, your fortune,
> and your fullness."*
> — Sri Sathya Sai Baba

The energy of love reverberates through the Universe. It is as prevalent as the air we breathe and every bit as life sustaining. Love is the source of creativity. It is the motivation of courage, the origin of kindness.

Love's energy is aroused through the experience of appreciation—from the tiniest flash of gratitude to the most profound recognition of value. If we open ourselves to the many places where love can be found—instead of just narrowing our perception to the romantic pursuit of love—we can enrich our lives beyond belief. And if it *is* romantic love that we're looking for, our choice to have a greater consciousness of our other experiences of love can only increase our likelihood of attracting it.

One of the worst things that you can do to your energy is to set limits on your potential for receiving love. This effectively blocks the current of power and joy that could be flowing into your life even now. Hopelessness over being uncoupled for too long is a cognitive wall. No matter what happens, you must believe in the abundance of love in the Universe. Be patient. Love your life, and more love will come into it.

In fact, your choice to observe all of the little signs of love in your life increases both the love in the Universe and your magnetic attraction of it. New and unexpected avenues of potential love are waiting for you in the unlimited, vibrating realm of time and space.

The Quantum Connection

In quantum physics, the *Uncertainty Principle* reveals that all the world exists in a state of pure potential, an infinite array of possibilities. Given the right set of causes, any one of these infinite possibilities could spark into being at any moment.

> *For us personally, and for all the world, there is an endless flow of events and opportunities. They move through our lives and through space and time. A little change in energy can create a major change in events; a slight shift in consciousness can create a dramatic alteration of possibilities.*

We all bring our own energy to this ever-unfolding Universal dance. Millions of frequencies come together, mingling, connecting—their resonances reverberating. This state of flux is charged with energy and action. At every moment options, possibilities, causes, and consequences come alive in unimaginable permutations. In the beat of a heart, in the flash of a thought, in one moment of action, everything changes.

In this kind of highly charged environment, *you need to know* that anything can happen—at any time—including the outcome of your desires. In any given moment, an infinite number of potential events could be excited into existence by virtue of your intention. When you change from within, everything around you changes, also.

This is the essence of the energetic world. The love of your life may be just around the corner. The solutions you seek may reveal themselves in the very next moment.

Whether you realize it or not, the energy of your consciousness has both immediate and distant power. This is the *non-local* nature of your quantum connection. The activity of your intentions can excite spontaneous and far-reaching results.

How often do you ask yourself what your consciousness is creating now? What personal or even distant events could you be shifting into place this very moment? While it's true that a higher, brighter energy of consciousness will attract better and brighter results for you personally, the process of cause and effect does not stop there.

Your energy expands in the Universe, connecting and collecting with other vibrating energies. All that you generate moves into great fields of similar consciousness. When enough energy accumulates, it exerts its influence far and wide.

Consciousness Fields Forever

Fields are often described as forces that exist in space and somehow influence the matter they surround. We can witness the gravitational and electromagnetic fields at work in the orbit of the earth around the sun and in the needle of a compass pointing north. But there's much more to the field phenomenon than that.

It's clear that our Personal Energy Field influences our own individual experience. What most people are unaware of, however, is that our personal energy also extends across the Universe and has significant consequences in the lives of others—even people we will never meet.

This global influence of individual energy is a function of what is called the *morphogenetic field* or the *M-field.* The word *morphogenetic* comes from two Greek words meaning "form" and "birth." Morphogenetics is the study of how forms come into being—not just physical forms, but behavior and thought-forms, also.

In his 1981 book *A New Science of Life,* British biologist Rupert Sheldrake explored how consciousness generates the force behind the *morphogenetic fields.* These are fields of energy and information that are fed by each individual within the species. Waves of thought and personal energy are poured into a group consciousness, an energetic field that reaches through time and space. Through the process that Sheldrake calls *morphic resonance,* the field builds momentum and in turn affects the development of the entire species. Specific knowledge and behavioral habits accumulate in the field. That accumulated consciousness expands, and when it achieves a critical magnitude, it moves into the awareness of everyone in the species.

Take, for example, the popularization of the personal computer. When it was developed, the operating systems were difficult to understand. Yet as more people became exposed, the systems became easier. The consciousness of computing expanded, and more and more people engaged in the experience, contributing their own personal energy to an ever-growing field of consciousness. Over just a few decades, the M-field of computer consciousness has expanded exponentially, getting easier and easier, reaching out to people of all ages, all walks of life, and virtually every culture and country on the globe.

Throughout time, we can see similar—though perhaps not as rapid—patterns of morphic resonance. The Renaissance of the 15th and 16th centuries brought incredible accomplishments in art, science, religion, and exploration. The Industrial Revolution of the 1800s saw such advances in machinery and production that it completely altered the way much of the world made its living. In the 1900s, the technological age changed the fields of communication, medicine, transportation, and business. Now the morphic resonance of the digital era allows people from different sides of the planet to communicate over the Internet using software programs as translators.

It's easy to see, through these and many other examples, how the process of morphic resonance moves our species along in very specific energetic directions. In each of these cases, entire movements were spread across the globe through a sort of energetic domino effect, where consciousness increased knowledge and knowledge increased consciousness, until it seemed that the movement took on a life of its own. But morphic resonance is not limited to the intellectual development of humankind. It's a very real factor in the emotional and behavioral trends of our species.

Planting the Fields of Love and Fear

There are two great fields of emotional consciousness that we as human beings have been feeding since our species was born. These are the fields of love and fear. We contribute to the consciousness of these fields through our own energetic choices, our beliefs, our thoughts, and our behaviors. We feed the field of love through every caring thought, compassionate feeling, and kind deed. We feed the field of fear with every judgmental thought, hateful feeling, and aggressive act—every single one.

> *Through the phenomenon of morphic resonance,*
> *each of the fields of love and fear accelerates its own*
> *energy in the Universe. Depending on how much love*
> *or fear we engage in as individuals, that particular*
> *emotion is perpetuated in the consciousness of the*
> *species.*

There are two fundamental ways we contribute to the energy of each of these fields. One is through our perception of ourselves. When we love and accept ourselves, we generously feed the field of love. When we engage in self-criticism or self-judgment, we perpetuate the energy of fear.

What is your perception of *yourself?* Do you value yourself and see your true potential? Or do you judge yourself and see yourself—and your future—as limited? Self-judgment, self-loathing, and self-criticism all add up to the same thing, incapacitating emotional and energetic paralysis. It is, without a doubt, the most counterproductive energy you could generate.

And this dynamic does not stop with just your life. We are all inextricably connected. Physicist David Bohm calls it a "quantum interconnectedness." Because your individual energy is shared in the consciousness field, the effects of your own self-treatment will, in time, belong to everybody.

The other fundamental way we feed these fields is through our acceptance or judgment of others. People judge because it makes them feel more powerful at the moment. But every time you make a judgment of another, the energy of judgment is redirected your way. *Whenever you judge, you tell yourself that judgment is acceptable. And if it's acceptable for you to judge, it's also acceptable for you to be judged.* This clearly promotes the energy of fear, worry, and competitiveness, not only in your own life, but also in the energy of the world.

Your choices do have power, not just for you, but for all of us. Your frequencies affect your family, your community, your culture, your country, your world. *You are—at every moment—participating in the expansion of a Universal energy.*

So you need to ask yourself, how do *you* participate? What are you contributing to our energetic world? What is the dominant energy of your daily life?

If you look around and want to know what you can do to help, your *self* is the best place to start. If you want to know what you can do to stop terrorism, stop terrorizing your self. If you want to know what you can do to stop abuse and neglect, stop abusing and neglecting your self.

Instead, work on expanding your own self-loving energy. Reconnect with your true and lovable self. Recognize your unalterable value, and you will recognize the value in others. Your consciousness is a viable source of the morphic resonance of our time. Your choices to love both yourself and others will expand the energy of Universal love and help to break down the consciousness of fear.

Fear is actually born out of our separation from our self and our spirit. Without being fully aware of our eternal power and intrinsic value, we naturally seek power and value in externals. Since we view the world as limited, we become afraid that others will threaten our achievement of those external things. It is this fear that makes us separate into groups. It makes us establish an "us/them" mentality. We seek strength in numbers, power in affiliation.

Group Consciousness

We affiliate in groups because we feel they can give us some sort of leverage in the external world. We make conclusions about the power and value of our group, then we compare that to the groups we perceive as competition. Some common examples of these comparisons are:

- "My family is richer than yours."

- "My culture is more worthy than yours."

- "My religion is more holy, more correct than yours."

- "My race is more valuable than yours."

- "My gender is more important than yours."

With enough repetition and enough people reinforcing them, these conclusions pick up energy and turn into *group consciousness*. These kinds of group mentalities are deadly to the intention of love and unification. They actually motivate us to promote the hostility in society through some skewed sense of loyalty to those groups with which we have affiliated.

The fervor over group importance increases with the passage of time. If it's a consciousness that has been embraced for decades or even centuries, its morphic resonance accelerates to such a degree that it could even determine significant historical events.

There have been entire eras that have resonated with group consciousness driven by fear and hate. The "Holy" Wars of the Crusades, the Inquisition, the practice of slavery, and the genocide of World War II are all examples of this consciousness brought into manifestation.

In each of these cases, fear created a desperate search for power and became the motivating force behind the choices of everyone who took part. This adversarial group consciousness imposed an assumption of superiority that was so profoundly embraced, this alone was used as justification for the violence imposed by one group upon another.

But a superiority mentality is not always the predominant energy of a group consciousness. For many groups, the opposite is true. Years of being treated brutally have shifted some groups into attitudes of inferiority and lack. It's a consciousness that's fed by conclusions born out of chronic mistreatment by other groups seeking power—conclusions such as:

- "My culture is always victimized."
- "My race is always abused."
- "My gender is always powerless."

As more and more people embrace these beliefs, their energy expands, causing their morphic resonance to accelerate and reach outward. The consciousness then takes hold more strongly, broadcasting its energetic influence to every member of the group—whether they're aware of it or not.

This is the group resonance, the race resonance, the gender resonance, the culture and religion resonance. There have been so many groups that have been made to believe that they're powerless and valueless—and destined to remain so.

But any consciousness can be changed. Each one of us can choose to see how our own personal resonance may be feeding the negative pattern. And then—through new beliefs and behaviors—we can make the shift ourselves.

Gender Resonance

One negative group consciousness that we can all help to change is the gender resonance of being female. All over the world, women have been subjugated and oppressed. For thousands of years, both genders and all races have contributed to the consciousness of the devalued woman.

And this consciousness continues to expand every time a woman is attacked, harassed, abused, or subjugated. Every event in the process—when not intervened upon—feeds the process itself. And the process, in turn, increases the resonance, which then encourages more events.

Yet every time a woman resists, intervenes, or takes some sort of action in her own behalf—even after the fact—she changes the resonance of that event by changing the consciousness of powerlessness. Her intention to take control, whether she's completely successful or not, says that it's no longer acceptable to abuse a woman. This intention, along with any action to support it, creates an energetic shift in the gender resonance. In fact, anytime anyone—man or woman—intervenes on any energy that devalues women, that consciousness is changed.

And every time a woman is treated with respect, every time she is prioritized and acknowledged as being equal, this too creates a shift in the gender consciousness. It reroutes the energy to a different mentality, a resonance of value and empowerment. Every time a woman walks away from hostility and rejects criticism, she feeds the new resonance even more. And every time we teach our children to treat each other with respect—no matter what the gender or race—we move each group consciousness even further into enlightenment and positive vibration.

> *Each and every group consciousness—whether it be gender, race, religious, or cultural—must change its adversarial energy. Assumptions of superiority and the need for control must be dropped. Conclusions of victimization and disempowerment must be turned around. The energy must be balanced. It is time to make a shift to* one *consciousness,* one *resonance that brings the same energy to all—value, authentic power, and love to all.*

As individuals, we must choose new thoughts and behaviors that release our group mentalities and embrace our *one global identity* instead. As more and more of us do this, the consciousness we are projecting will change, and it will become a group decision to let go of the old, fearful energy that used to separate us.

It's time for us to recognize our unmistakable, unbreakable connection. It's time to see that there's far more value and strength in joining together than in pursuing this persistent need for separation. It's time to embrace each other—all of us— as valued and equal partners in the business of destiny creation.

Life no longer needs to be an unending competition where somebody wins and somebody else loses. Our authentic power is increased when everyone wins. We can rejoice at the joys of others because we know that joyous energy, like any resonance that is repeated, expands to all.

Jesus did not say, "Love thy group." He did not say, "Love thy neighbor if they are the same race, the same gender, the same religion." In saying, "Love thy neighbor as thyself," he was revealing even then the defining connection, the "quantum interconnectedness" between us all.

The flame of God's presence is the same within everybody. It doesn't change with different colors or different sexes. It's neither too fat nor too thin. It's not rich or poor, well dressed or shabby. It is only Divine, and it is the same Divine light in each and every one of us.

You can see this light in the people you encounter. As you pass them on the street, allow yourself to disregard the outward signals you might have paid attention to before. Instead, look for the light that lives within each person. See it sparkle in their eyes and radiate from their hearts. Bless that light and thank it for its presence.

When you do this, you will see passionately. A radical joy will fill your life. It will be impossible to focus either on personal lack or separation from others. Your intention to see love and spread it will make your entire life romantic.

The Romantic Life

You don't have to limit the romance in your life to your pursuit of a relationship. The Universe is filled with it. When you make the choice to see your life with loving eyes, you will uncover romance on a daily—even hourly—basis.

It's your attitude that creates the romance in your life, the ability to embrace all the tenderness there. When you move through your days taking notice, feeling the gentility, seeing the beauty, then passion and joy will become the norm, not just the exception.

You are the key. Your intention opens the door. Look around you. God is sending you flowers. The Universe is asking you for a date. The diamond stars are there for your engagement.

You will draw more joy and romance to you by creating a life intention to conduct your own loving energy to others. *Love is such an easy, fluid, and yet powerful vibration, it can be sent with just your intention to do so.*

You are a generator, a transmitter, and also a receiver. Open your heart center, smile, and send out great waves of light and love to the hearts of people you encounter. Wake up in the morning and affirm, "I am sending love to all I see today." Then gently do it everywhere you go.

Every day you can make love with your life. See a gift in the sunset. Enjoy an embrace from a warm summer's breeze. Feel the kiss of the Divine in every beat of your heart. Celebrate your anniversary with life each day. Make every moment a meditation on the miracle that is you.

The degree to which you love your life and value yourself is your ultimate *secret of attraction.* This is your energetic truth. It's not a selfish love, but an authentic appreciation that finally sets you free. Open yourself to the love in your heart, and you'll soon become aware of the love all around you.

You are the cosmic mirror. If you are willing to shift your energy, the Universe will reflect that. Your repeated intention to love has an impact on the frequency and current of all the loving energy in the world. Always remember: *No truly loving word or behavior—whether it's towards yourself or someone else—can fail to receive a beneficial response in the resonant state.*

The ever-expanding field of love is waiting for your input, waiting to see how you look at yourself in the mirror, waiting to see what you think of yourself and how you treat yourself through the day. Know that the love that you deliver to it, you're not only delivering to yourself, but also to the hurt and lonely hearts around the world. Think about this and then ask yourself, "What is my energetic choice—this moment, this hour, this day?"

The world is ready to be healed. We must bring our love and reverence to every living thing—every group, every person, and every creature on the planet—starting with ourselves and our family, all the way to the planet itself.

Take your time. There's no hurry. There's no competition. The only race is the human race. And the power of Divine Love flows through every single heart within it. How you connect with one—or all—of those hearts will depend on how you connect with your own. Choose to see the love and the beauty there, and you will magnetize love and beauty everywhere.

It's all up to you now. The light and energy, the causes and consequences of all the world are ever changing, constantly in flow. You live in a world of pure potential, ***and the return of your own energy never, ever stops.***

Excite your heart! *Feel* the power of joyous anticipation fill every cell of your being. With certainty in your worth—and honoring in your intentions—release your desires to the abundant Universe. Live with joy and wait with patience for the wonderful returns.

Your soul is at play in the garden of endless possibilities. Sow the seeds of a radiant and loving resonance, and you will harvest an eternity of brilliant bouquets!

❧ AFTERWORD ❧

IN HIS BOOK *QUANTUM REALITY,* Nick Herbert tells a great story about Niels Bohr, a brilliant quantum physicist, which goes something like this: A visitor to Bohr's country home noticed a horseshoe over the door. Utterly surprised, the visitor asked if Bohr could believe in such a good-luck superstition. Bohr responded, "Of course I don't believe in it. But you know, they say that it works whether you believe in it or not."

Such are the Laws of Attraction. They're founded in the energy dynamics of our physical world. And they're a powerful presence whether you believe in them or not. Since their effects are as certain as the law of gravity, it would be valuable to be ever-mindful of their influence.

Law Review

The core of the Law of Magnetism is self-honoring. There's no getting around this; it's the absolute bare minimum of change that you must make if you want to truly alter your destiny. All of the other laws—and the Universe itself—respond to this energetic dimension of your life. No genuine happiness can spring from the heart of a person who does not recognize and celebrate their own intrinsic value.

The keys to the Law of Pure Desire are belief and surrender. Without belief, you can't hope to connect with the flow of real love. Without surrender, your urgency will sabotage everything that you go after. For this reason, the Law of Paradoxical Intent requires trust. You must trust that you can create happiness in your own life, and then take the action to do so. Your choice to be happy no matter what, magnetizes happiness no matter what.

The fundamentals of the Law of Harmony are releasing judgment and choosing to see the equal hearts and souls of all people. Your love of others creates much more of that loving energy than just an equal amount in the world. Every loving act or thought multiplies itself many thousandfold. The energy of love seeks to expand, and given even just a start in your heart, it will do so.

You can never get too much positive energy in your life. Now is the time to prioritize your energy production. Develop a strong awareness of the kind of energy that you're creating, and work on the skills that you know will help. Review your options often, and see if you can add even more techniques to your repertoire. Whatever you do, remember the basic requirements of the laws. These are absolutes and can't be dismissed in your desire to create a joyous resonance.

The Law of Magnetism

- Watch what you really believe about yourself— you're going to magnetize someone who believes the same thing.

- Be silent; meditate. It creates a peaceful, attractive frequency because it connects you with the timeless value of your soul.

- Cultivate and revel in your Grand Relationship. The Divine is the source of all real love.

- Use honoring language. Affirm yourself and your life. Amplify your affirmations by speaking them out loud. *Never stop affirming,* and you'll never stop attracting affirmative experiences.

- Intervene on your toxic, negative, or fearful

thoughts. When in doubt about what to think, always choose optimism!

- Whenever you make a decision or choose a course of action, ask yourself, "Does this honor me?" Then muster up the courage to do the honoring thing.

- Always know that you're in the process of creating and projecting energy. Think about this and ask yourself, "Is the energy I'm creating now the kind of energy I want to attract back into my life?" If it isn't, *change it!*

The Law of Pure Desire

- Allow yourself to pursue your desires wholeheartedly. Just make sure that they're not fear-based, but motivated out of love.

- Affirm that you already have what you're hoping for. Let your hopes become your beliefs.

- Believe that you're worthy of receiving. Know that you deserve to be happy and to attract great things.

- Excite the energy of your desires. Visualize that which you wish to happen; *feel* the excitement and appreciation fill you up with wonderful emotions. Do this often, and those emotions will become real for you.

- Surrender your attachment to the outcome. Don't invest any of your identity or worth in its achievement. Let it go with trust. The Universe is willing to work for you if you're willing to be patient and trust.

- Be open to the options. Don't obsess about only one outcome; this will stop you cold. The Universe is abundant and offers an abundance of opportunities for happiness. Be open to them.

The Law of Paradoxical Intent

- Be very clear about your intentions. If your intention is to be happy, making yourself miserable obsessing about a goal will certainly not create the happiness you're looking for.

- Be careful not to fall into desperation. Desperation is poison to desire and only ends up pushing it away.

- Watch your constructs. Anytime you attach your happiness, value, or worth to an external, you sabotage your intention. Create your happiness now. Know that you're worthy now. Affirm your value in every moment, and value will return.

- Appreciate all that you have in your life. Stop obsessing about what you lack.

- Let go of the urgency. Urgency is fear-based and discounts your potential for being happy now. Surrender your need to control the future. Your greatest gift is in the present— don't let your desire throw that gift away.

The Law of Harmony

- Forge a loving relationship with the Universe— and with everyone and everything in it. This increases your love and power to the very degree that you do it.

- Live a life of balance. Create balance in your own lifestyle—in your energy, activity, and consumption. Balance others' needs with yours. Honoring yourself honors them; honoring others enriches you.

- See yourself as equal, with the same value as all. See others as equal, too. When you stop competing, you start manifesting.

- Look for opportunities to show compassion. Always know that your fellow human being shares an identity with you. We are all connected, children in the family of God, one in the consciousness of man.

- Be of service—not out of guilt or obligation, but out of a pure desire to show love.

- Live with reverence. All of life is sacred. So let go of your judgment and your need to separate. With unity comes real peace and the ultimate manifestation of everyone's desires.

Never give up on your dreams. You *do* have the power to make them a reality. In fact, you have all of the power of the Universe at your disposal. Bring your loving energy to it and it will bless you with unending love in return.

❧ SUGGESTED READING ❧

Beyond the Quantum, Michael Talbot. New York, NY: Bantam, 1988.

The Dancing Wu Li Masters, Gary Zukav. New York, NY: Quill, 1979.

Emotional Intelligence, Daniel Goleman. New York, NY: Bantam, 1995.

Energy Medicine, Donna Eden. New York, NY: Putnam, 1998.

Equations of Eternity, David Darling. New York, NY: Hyperion, 1993.

The Holographic Paradigm, Ed. Ken Wilber. Boston, New Science Library, 1985.

The Holographic Universe, Michael Talbot. New York, NY: HarperCollins, 1991.

The Holotropic Mind, Stanislav Grof with Hal Zina Bennett. New York, NY: HarperCollins, 1993.

Learned Optimism, Martin Seligman. New York, NY: Pocket Books, 1992.

The Living Energy Universe, Gary Schwartz & Linda Russek. Charlottesville, VA: Hampton Roads, 1999.

Manifest Your Destiny, Dr. Wayne W. Dyer. New York, NY: Harper Paperbacks, 1997.

Miracles of Mind, Russell Targ & Jane Katra. Novato, California: New World Library, 1998.

Mysticism and the New Physics, Michael Talbot. New York, NY: Penguin, 1981.

The Numinous Universe, Daniel Liderbach. New York, NY: Paulist Press, 1989.

Other Worlds, Paul Davies. New York, NY: Penguin, 1988.

Parallel Universe, Fred Alan Wolf. New York, NY: Touchstone, 1988.

The Physics of Immortality, Frank J. Tipler. New York, NY: Doubleday, 1994.

Quantum Reality, Nick Herbert. New York, NY: Anchor, 1985.

The Quantum Self, Danah Zohar. New York, NY: Quill, 1990.

The Seat of the Soul, Gary Zukav. New York, NY: Fireside, 1990.

The Seven Spiritual Laws of Success, Deepak Chopra. New York, NY: New World Library, 1994.

Soul Stories, Gary Zukav. New York, NY: Fireside, 2000.

The Spiritual Universe, Fred Alan Wolf. Portsmouth, NH: Moment Point Press, 1999.

Taking the Quantum Leap, Fred Alan Wolf. New York, NY: Harper and Row, 1989.

❧ ABOUT THE AUTHOR ❧

Sandra Anne Taylor has been a counselor in a private psychological practice for 22 years. She lectures internationally on the energetic laws of manifestation, the quantum mechanics of consciousness, and psycho-spiritual healing. Sandra lives in the Cleveland area with her husband and two children.

Also available from Sandra Anne Taylor are the following *guided visualization* tapes:

Attracting Love—The companion tape to this book, a guided imagery process designed to project your highest and best energy and to help you magnetize your ideal partner.

Your Sacred Identity—Realigning with the peace and power of your true, eternal self.

Relaxation and Memory Release—Letting go of the tension of past or present problems.

Cellular Regression: Timeless Healing—Regressing your cells back to their original, Divine, and healthy state.

Higher Self, Higher Powers—Turning to the power of your higher self for any quality or strength you will ever need.

Planting Your Destiny Garden—Sowing the seeds of a brilliant and abundant destiny.

Successful Weight Loss—Visualization and affirmations to achieve your ideal weight.

Now available on an eight-tape audio program—
Sandra's popular and life-changing seminar:

Life Magic!
Manifest Your Deepest Desires
Through Cosmic Power and Law

This audio seminar explores in detail the five creative powers, the four laws of attraction, and the seven energy changes that will truly revolutionize your life. Untold Universal energy is at your disposal. Learn to tap into it. Achieve your greatest goals, and change your life forever.

To order tapes, log-on to: **www.sandrataylor.net.**

To schedule a lecture, seminar, or private consultation with Sandra, call: (440) 356-9141, or write to her at:
P.O. Box 362, Avon, Ohio 44011.

❧❀ ❀⊕❀ ❀❧

Notes

Notes

$\mathcal{N}otes$

Notes

We hope you enjoyed this Hay House book.
If you'd like to receive our online catalog featuring additional information on
Hay House books and products, or if you'd like to find out more about the
Hay Foundation, please contact:

Hay House, Inc.
P.O. Box 5100
Carlsbad, CA 92018-5100

(760) 431-7695 or **(800) 654-5126**
(760) 431-6948 (fax) or **(800) 650-5115 (fax)**
www.hayhouse.com® • **www.hayfoundation.org**

Published and distributed in Australia by:
Hay House Australia Pty. Ltd., 18/36 Ralph St., Alexandria NSW 2015
Phone: 612-9669-4299 • *Fax:* 612-9669-4144 • www.hayhouse.com.au

Published and distributed in the United Kingdom by: Hay House UK, Ltd., 292B Kensal Rd.,
London W10 5BE • *Phone:* 44-20-8962-1230 • *Fax:* 44-20-8962-1239 www.hayhouse.co.uk

Published and distributed in the Republic of South Africa by:
Hay House SA (Pty), Ltd., P.O. Box 990, Witkoppen 2068 • *Phone/Fax:* 27-11-467-8904
info@hayhouse.co.za • www.hayhouse.co.za

Published in India by: Hay House Publishers India,
Muskaan Complex, Plot No. 3, B-2, Vasant Kunj, New Delhi 110 070
Phone: 91-11-4176-1620 • *Fax:* 91-11-4176-1630 • www.hayhouse.co.in

Distributed in Canada by: Raincoast, 9050 Shaughnessy St., Vancouver, B.C. V6P 6E5
Phone: (604) 323-7100 • *Fax:* (604) 323-2600 • www.raincoast.com

Take Your Soul on a Vacation

Visit **www.HealYourLife.com®** to regroup, recharge, and reconnect with your
own magnificence. Featuring blogs, mind-body-spirit news, and life-changing
wisdom from Louise Hay and friends.

Visit **www.HealYourLife.com** today!

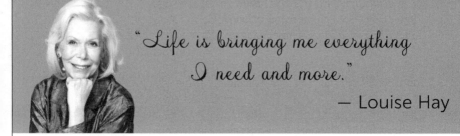